Corfu

Original text by Donna Dailey
Revised by Paul Murphy
Updated by Donna Dailey
Editor: Jeffery Pike
Managing Editor: Clare Peel
Series Editor: Tony Halliday

Berlitz® POCKET GUIDE

Corfu

Fifth Edition 2004
Updated 2006

PHOTOGRAPHY
AKG-images London 13; Elizabeth Boleman-Herring 1, 6, 11, 22, 24, 26, 38, 39, 45, 48, 54, 69, 71, 75, 77, 80, 83, 85, 87, 89, 95, 96, 99, 100; Donna Dailey 21, 42, 51; Glyn Genin 16; Paul Murphy 10, 15, 30, 31, 32, 34, 35, 36, 47, 52, 55, 56, 58, 61, 65, 67, 68, 72, 76, 79, 82, 91, 93; Topham Picturepoint 18; Phil Wood 29, 41; Gregory Wrona 9.
Cover: M.F. Chillmaid/Robert Harding.

CONTACTING THE EDITORS
Every effort has been made to provide accurate information in this publication, but changes are inevitable. The publisher cannot be responsible for any resulting loss, inconvenience or injury. We would appreciate it if readers would call our attention to any errors or outdated information by contacting Berlitz Publishing, PO Box 7910, London SE1 1WE, England.
Fax: (44) 20 7403 0290;
e-mail: berlitz@apaguide.co.uk
www.berlitzpublishing.com

The northeast coast of Corfu (page 57) is particularly beautiful, with rocky coves and traditional fishing villages

The massive Gorgon pediment dominates Kérkyra Town's Archaeological Museum (page 40)

Paleokastrítsa (page 66) is the island's most famous beauty spot

TOP TEN ATTRACTIONS

The fine Byzantine Museum (page 34) is housed in a 15th-century basilica ▼

The grandiose Achilleion Palace (page 46) is one of the most visited sights on the island ◄

The west coast (page 70) is noted for its glorious sandy beaches, including those at Glyfáda, right, and Myrtiótissa ►

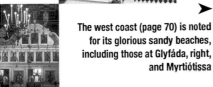

The elegant Liston (page 31) in Kérkyra Town was modelled on the Rue de Rivoli in Paris ▼

► The massive fortress of Angelókastro (page 68) dates from the 13th century

Take a day trip to the charming island of Paxí (page 73) ◄

The monastery on Mt Pandokrátor (page 57) houses many ancient frescoes and icons ◄

CONTENTS

Fact Sheets

INTRODUCTION

Swathed in a blanket of deep green, its mountainous sky-line plunging into a crystal-clear, turquoise sea, Corfu is known as Greece's Emerald Island. It is not only among the lushest of Greece's myriad islands but one of the prettiest as well. Flowering bushes, shrubs and trees cloak most of its rolling landscape, and in spring the island is bursting with beautiful wild flowers.

Corfu's sunny beaches, spectacular scenery and charming capital have enchanted visitors – including many writers and artists – throughout the centuries. The wonderful clear light and stunning vistas of the island are thought to have been the inspiration for settings in Homer's *Odyssey* and Shakespeare's *Tempest*. In more recent times, the British poet and painter Edward Lear depicted many views of Corfu's now famous sights, while the authors Lawrence and Gerald Durrell both lived here and wrote entertaining books about island life. Many past celebrities, from the Rothschilds to the Greek royal family and the empress of Austria, have had villas built on the island. This tradition continues today, with many an Italian industrial magnate retreating to Corfu.

Secluded Resorts

Since the late 1970s, Corfu has become known as a popular British playground: over half of all the island's holiday visitors come from the UK. No doubt early visitors felt very much at home sipping ginger beer and watching cricket matches in Kérkyra Town (Corfu Town) – both relics of British rule (1814–64) that can still be enjoyed today. The more recent introduction of cheap package tourism in the 1980s gave Corfu something of a reputation as a 'party island'. However, the party scene was always restricted to a few enclaves, and over the last few years some of those have mellowed considerably. Nonetheless, there are definitely still a few places that are best avoided by anyone who prefers the atmosphere of a Greek island to a rowdy British seaside town.

In keeping with island character and scale, many resorts are small, quiet and secluded. Though development has been rapid on some parts of the island, it is still much less overbearing than in many other Mediterranean vacation destinations. In marked contrast to the European mainland, there are no high-rise horrors and only the occasional large hotel. Actually, much of the island remains untouched by mass tourism, and the main resorts are really crowded only in July and August. Remarkably, even in peak season you can still find secluded places for sunbathing and hiking along the coastline and throughout the hilly hinterland. You just have to make that little bit of effort (usually either on foot or by boat) to get there.

> Language is no problem for most visitors. Many locals speak English or Italian, and most signs are posted in both Greek and Roman characters.

Location and Size

Corfu is the most northerly of the Ionian group of islands. Just across the water to the east are Albania and the Greek mainland. Only 74km (46 miles) to the northwest is Italy. To the south are the delightful island of Paxí and the other Ionians (Lefkáda, Itháki, Kefalloniá, Zákynthos and Kýthira); However, island-hopping is an option only for travellers with lots of time on their hands.

Corfu is also Greece's western gateway and has proudly styled itself 'the entry to the Adriatic'. It is no coincidence that the Ottomans – who conquered the rest of mainland Greece and its islands – failed to gain a foothold here. Instead, it was the great Western European powers of the day

(Venice, France and Britain) who left their mark during five centuries of island occupation. Nowhere is this more noticeable than in the elegant architecture and cosmopolitan atmosphere of Kérkyra Town. Where else in the world could you sit at a French-style café, amid Venetian streets, sipping Greek coffee while watching English cricket? This stylish capital is regarded as the loveliest town in all the Greek islands, and a visit here is a highlight of most visitors' holidays.

In its shape Corfu resembles a scythe, measuring about 65km (40 miles) in

The elegant arcade of the Liston

length and ranging in width from 4km to 30km (2½ miles to 19 miles). According to geologists, the island is the exposed crown of a submerged mountain range that broke off eons ago from the mainland to the east. The highest point is Mt Pandokrátor, really only a fairly modest-sized peak of just over 900m (2,950ft). But on this relatively small island it takes on much more importance, and the summit is approached only by an impressive ascent along steep hairpin bends.

Hire a car, if only for a few days. No matter where you are based, you can very easily get around and explore the whole island. As you tour Corfu you'll see on the undulating hills and stone-hedged terraces silvery groves of prized

A traditional house

olive trees – venerable, knotted and gnarled. In the past they were an economic lifeline for the island, and they still provide excellent olive oil, and wood for carving souvenirs. The island is also graced with legions of orange and lemon trees (giving off a glorious aroma in spring), plane trees, jacaranda, palms, wisteria, myrtle and oleander. Even the simplest homes are adorned with verdant grape arbours and enormous, beautiful clusters of roses or bougainvillea. Most memorable of all are the groves of tall, slim cypresses rising like sentries on the hillsides.

Visit in spring or early summer if possible to see the best of the island's flora: there are 100 native wild flowers alone that grow nowhere else. You might get a little wet then, but it's a price worth paying. The reason for Corfu's remarkably luxuriant vegetation is that more rain falls here – trapped by the nearby mainland mountains – than in any other part of Greece. However, for most of the year this is very much an island in the sun.

Clean Beaches, Casual Living

Corfu has about 200km (124 miles) of coastline with some of Europe's most beautiful and cleanest beaches. They vary from strips of pure golden sand to bright white pebbles and stones to combinations of all three. While swells for surfing can be found on the western shores, there are plenty of calm bays suitable for all the family on the more protected east coast. As for the sea itself, in any one cove the range of clear blues seems to defy the colour spectrum. Don't miss a day trip to the Diapóndia islets or Andípaxi, where the waters are as clear as those in the Caribbean.

Just over 100,000 people live on Corfu. Some of them emigrate – attracted by life abroad or in the big mainland cities – but countless others have never left the island. Instead, the world comes to them, in increasing numbers that today reach one million annually. Yet despite the seasonal influx of visitors, the inhabitants on the whole retain a fresh, open simplicity that delights visitors.

Life on Corfu is cool, casual and unhurried. For the punctilious northern European visitor it can sometimes be a bit too casual: waiting for the bus that is 20 minutes late (or never comes); the 'fast-food' kebab for which you have to queue for 15 minutes; the restaurant order that takes an eternity, then arrives cold. Be patient and remember that nobody ever came to Corfu (or anywhere else in Greece, for that matter) for Swiss service, French food or Scandinavian plumbing. After all, the slow pace of life here is the key to both *filoxenía* (traditional Greek hospitality to strangers) and *filótimo* (sense of honour).

Finding time for refreshment

A BRIEF HISTORY

Little is known about Corfu's first inhabitants. Prehistoric traces found at Gardhíki in the southwest date back to the Palaeolithic Era (70,000BC to 40,000BC), when the island was probably joined to the Greek mainland. But unlike on other Ionian islands, no traces of Mycenaean settlements have ever surfaced on Corfu, leading to speculation that the island might have been held by the Phoenicians during that period (1500BC to 1150BC).

Corfu's acknowledged history begins in 734BC, when the Corinthians established a colony called Corcyra south of

Ulysses and the Stone Ship

According to Homer's *Odyssey*, the hero Ulysses ('Odysseus' in Greek) was shipwrecked during his 10-year voyage home from the Trojan War. He was washed ashore on the island of Schería – the ancient name of Corfu – which was inhabited by people known as Phaeacians. There he was found by Princess Nausikaa and her hand-maidens when they came to wash clothes at a nearby stream. She persuaded her father, King Alkinous, to provide a boat to return him to his native Ithaca, but this assistance angered Poseidon (the god of the sea), who turned the ship to stone.

Three Corfu sites claim a starring role as the place described in Homer's epic poem where Ulysses' boat was petrified. All have the requisite double harbour approached by a narrow causeway, as well as an offshore rock that (with a good dose of imagination) resembles a petrified ship. These are Mouse Island, off Kanóni; Kolóvri, off Paleokastrítsa; and Krávia (meaning 'ship'), northwest of Cape Arílla. The beach where Ulysses was washed ashore is said to be the west coast's Érmones, largely on account of its small stream.

today's Kérkyra Town in an area known as Paleópolis (Old City). Archaeological digs (still in progress) have turned up evidence of temples near Kardáki Spring and Mon Repos, but the ancient city was otherwise destroyed by barbarian raiders, its stone blocks used to build medieval Kérkyra Town. The famous 6th-century BC Gorgon pediment from the Temple of Artemis, now in the Archaeological Museum, is the single most important surviving artefact of classical Corcyra.

Odysseus and Nausikaa depicted by Allesandro Allori

Prospering from trade with southern Italy, Corcyra set up its own colonies on the nearby mainland and grew into a strong maritime power. In 665BC, Corcyra defeated Corinth in what the historian Thucydides described as the first naval battle in Greek history. Thus did Corfu gain its independence from the mainland.

Corfu's pact with Athens against Corinth and Sparta in 433BC proved to be, according to Thucydides, the final straw that set off the Peloponnesian War and brought about the end of classical Greece. From then on, Corfu suffered attack, pillage and often highly destructive occupation. Situated only 74km (46 miles) from Italy and barely 2km (1 mile) from the Albanian and Greek mainland at its nearest point, Corfu's safe harbours, fertile soil and strategic position between the Adriatic and Ionian seas made it a prize worth contesting by the many powers fighting for control of the region.

Roman Conquest

Around 230BC a Roman fleet arrived and took over control of the island, making Corfu the Roman Empire's earliest Adriatic conquest. For the next five and a half centuries, Corfu prospered as a Roman naval base used for forays into the mainland. En route to and from battles – or simply as tourists – Nero, Tiberius, Cato, Cicero, Caesar, Octavian and Mark Antony (with Cleopatra) were among the Roman notables who visited Corfu. During the 1st century AD two saints – Iáson (Jason) and Sosípatros (Sosipater) – brought Christianity to the island. Certain structures at Paleópolis, on the road to Kanóni, are among the few remnants from Corfu's Roman period.

When the Roman Empire split in the 4th century AD, its eastern half, Byzantium, took administrative control of Corfu but could provide little security. Rampaging Vandals raided the island in 445 and worse was to follow: in 562 a horde of Ostrogoths savagely destroyed Corfu's ancient capital.

After foiling an attempted takeover by Slavs in 933, the Corfiots moved their capital 2km (1 mile) north and built their first fortress on the rocky bluff commanding the town's eastern sea approach. The Old Fort still stands today on this site. Elsewhere, islanders abandoned coastal settlements and retreated inland to establish protected hillside villages.

Normans and Sicilians

Then appeared a formidable new enemy. Several times between 1080 and 1185 Norman forces crossed the Ionian Sea from Sicily to attack Corfu and nearby island outposts of the enfeebled Byzantine Empire. The rulers in Constantinople asked for help, the Venetians responded and thereafter took an active interest in the destiny of this Adriatic gateway island.

When Doge Enrico Dandolo and the crusaders conquered Constantinople in 1204, the spoils claimed by Venice included western Greece, parts of the Peloponnese, and the Ionian islands. But Venice was unable to extend immediate control over all its new holdings, and Corfu aligned itself with the Greek Despotate of Epirus, which then controlled parts of what are today Albania and western Greece. In 1214 Mikhaïl Ángelos Komnenós II, head of the despotate, took control of the island, leaving as a legacy the fortresses of Angelókastro and Gardhíki.

However, Sicily also had designs on Corfu. In 1259, to avoid all-out war, the island was presented to King Manfred, the Hohenstaufen king of Sicily, as his daughter's dowry. Eight years later, the new king of Sicily and Naples, Charles d'Anjou, became the overlord of Corfu, where his family – the Angevins – subsequently ruled for over a century. During this time the traditional Eastern Orthodoxy of the island was almost extinguished by the new official religion of Roman Catholicism.

A relic of Byzantine rule: the church of Ágii Iáson and Sosípatros

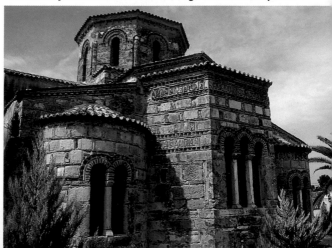

Venetian Rule

Venice's Lion of St Mark

As the Angevin dynasty ended and its hold on the island diminished, Corfu's fledgling assembly of 24 barons, mindful of the danger presented by marauding corsairs, invited Venice to send in a protective military force. The Venetians landed on 20 May 1386, beginning an occupation that was to last without interruption for over four centuries. In the following year, Corfu officially became part of the Stato da Mar, the Venetian maritime empire.

Corfu prospered once again as a key port for galleys plying far-flung commercial routes. To strengthen the defences of its harbour, the Venetians turned the Byzantine fort in Kérkyra Town into an impregnable bastion – a wise move.

In 1463, having swept across mainland Greece, the Ottoman Turks declared war on Venice. During the following years they mounted many assaults on the Ionian Islands, and in 1537 they turned on Corfu. Intent on seizing Kérkyra Town, the Ottoman fleet, led by the pirate-admiral Khair-el-Din (Barbarossa), a Greek renegade from Lésvos, landed cannons and 25,000 troops north of the capital at Gouviá. The fortress withstood a bitter attack, which became legendary in Corfiot history, but the rest of the island was looted and the vengeful Turks carried off some 15,000 to 20,000 prisoners – nearly half the population. Most of them were bound into slavery.

Following this great siege, the Venetians dug the Contrafossa, a canal separating the Old Fort from the town. They also erected a 'New Fortress' (so called even today) to guard the city's northwestern approach.

Corfu's finest military hour was to come in 1716, once more against the Turks and once more at great cost. After losing both Athens and the Peloponnese to the Venetians, the Ottoman sultan successfully counterattacked, retaking some of the Ionian islands and sending 30,000 troops to besiege Corfu. Venice had hired foreign regiments under the German mercenary commander Johann Matthias von der Schulenburg to defend the island. For six bloody weeks the troops held out in Kérkyra Town. The Turks, with their overwhelmingly superior forces, ravaged the rest of the island. They appeared to be ready to capture the capital when they suddenly called off their assault and fled, apparently frightened away by a ferocious thunder-and-hail storm.

> It is said that when the Turks attacked the island on 11 August 1716, St Spyrídon appeared with a lighted torch and scared the invaders away. That day is now one of the days that commemorate St Spyrídon, Corfu's patron saint *(see page 37)*.

The Turks did not return, and Corfu (along with all the other Ionian isles, save Lefkáda) was the only part of Greece never to be subjugated by the Ottomans.

Throughout its long feudal occupation, Venice kept Corfu under a strict regime, a colony valued as an important naval base, trading depot, customs-collection station and supply centre. A civil-military governor and senior bureaucrats sent from Venice ran the island. Much like Venice's Libro d'Oro, a Golden Book listing the Corfiot nobility contained 277 families at the time that Corfu passed from Venetian hands to Napoleonic forces.

However, ordinary islanders were heavily taxed and denied public education. Nothing was done to restore the Greek Orthodox religion to its traditional dominance among the faithful people. Italian replaced Greek as the official

Corfu became part of Napoleon's empire

language, even though the peasantry couldn't understand it and had no way of learning it. Many laboured as serfs in the Venetian aristocrats' villas, some of which still dot the countryside.

More happily, Venice was responsible for nearly all the olive trees that grace Corfu's landscape. Eager to ensure a constant supply of oil, the republic at one stage decreed a cash bonus for every 100 trees planted. Olive production transformed the island's economy for good. Apart from the olive trees, the most visible legacy of Venetian rule are the older districts of Kérkyra Town: with its narrow streets and tall buildings, it is the most Venetian town in Greece.

Napoleon's Dream Island

In 1797 the republic of the doges fell to Napoleon, thus ending 411 years of Venetian occupation. For reasons that remain obscure, Napoleon was rather obsessed with Corfu. 'The greatest misfortune which could befall me is the loss of Corfu,' he wrote rather melodramatically to his foreign minister, Talleyrand. So, immediately after capturing Venice, Napoleon sent a force to occupy Corfu and the other Ionian Islands.

These French occupiers replaced Venice's autocratic rule with new democratic representation, burned Corfu's Golden Book, introduced public education and made Greek the official language. Nevertheless, they still managed to antagonise the island's inhabitants by continuing to suppress the Orthodox

Church. Within two years the French were driven out of the island by a joint Russo-Turkish force that reinstated Greek Orthodoxy as the official religion under the puppet 'Septinsular Republic'. However, in 1807 the French regained Corfu from the Russians by the Treaty of Tilsit. This time Napoleon – never actually able to visit the island he'd called 'the key to the Adriatic' – garrisoned the citadels with 50,000 men along with 500 new cannons, making Corfu one of the most powerfully fortified points in the eastern Mediterranean.

The French brought many other bonuses to Corfu. They established the first Ionian Academy for the promotion of arts and sciences, imported Greece's first printing presses, drew up a street plan for Corfu Town, built a miniature Rue de Rivoli (the Liston) and began the growing of potatoes and tomatoes, now mainstays of Corfiot cooking.

The First European

Corfu's most famous son is Ioánnis Kapodístrias (1776–1831). Born of a noble family, he became Greece's first president in 1827 and is hailed as the first statesman to envisage a unified Europe.

With the collapse of the Venetian Empire in 1797, Kapodístrias was instrumental in the creation of the short-lived Federation of Ionian Islands. He then served as a diplomat in the Russian court of Tsar Alexander. On a mission to Switzerland in 1813, he orchestrated the Swiss Federation, which has remained in place to this day.

In the ensuing years he began to develop ideas of a unified Europe in which no one member would become too powerful and in which the powers would collectively regulate the whole. In this vision he was a man ahead of his time. Sadly, his political ideals also brought him parochial enemies, and he was assassinated on the Greek mainland in 1831 by two clan chieftains. In 1994 his home island fittingly hosted a summit meeting of the very union of which he had dreamed.

The British Move In

Napoleon's luck finally ran out. After his defeat at Waterloo, the British took Corfu in 1814. A year later, the Treaty of Vienna turned the seven Ionian Islands into one independent state under British protection. Corfu became the capital and Sir Thomas Maitland was appointed the state's Lord High Commissioner.

The British occupation of Corfu lasted for just 50 years, and brought certain benefits. Under Maitland, a road network was built. His successor, Frederick Adam, built the road to Paleokastrítsa and brought a permanent water-supply system to Kérkyra Town. While some changes were mere personal caprice on the part of the 10 British high commissioners, they also introduced new hospitals, model prisons, a decent judiciary, and religious freedom, ensuring the primacy of the Orthodox Church. The slightly eccentric Lord Guilford – a philhellene who went about in Classical Greek dress – established modern Greece's first university, the second Ionian Academy, in Kérkyra Town in 1824. He bequeathed to it his library of 25,000 books and helped to make Corfu the country's chief literary and intellectual centre of its day.

The constitution set in place by Maitland was another matter. Though maintaining a façade of parliamentary government with a Corfiot senate and assembly, the high commissioner maintained all effective power. Serious unrest first occurred in the 1820s, when Maitland stopped the Corfiots from giving assistance to their Greek mainland compatriots engaged in a war of independence against Turkey. This engendered bitterness among the islanders, who dubbed Maitland 'the abortion' for his rudeness, and aversion to bathing.

The British left behind a number of stately buildings and monuments as well as cricket, ginger beer and Christmas chutney – island favourites even today.

As a strong movement for unification with the mainland arose after Greece won independence in 1828, the British introduced token constitutional reforms (freeing the press and liberalising election procedures), but the high commissioner's power remained intact. However, agitation for union – *énosis* – continued to grow, until even the most stubborn colonialist saw the writing on the wall.

Statue of Frederick Adam

Greek at Last

When the pro-British Prince William of Denmark was crowned King George I in Athens in 1864, Corfu and the six other Ionian Islands were ceded to Greece as a gesture of goodwill to the new monarch. An agreement drawn up by the major powers of the day declared the islands 'perpetually neutral', and, before hauling down the Union Jack, the British blew up the impressive fortifications they had added to Kérkyra Town. When they sailed off, the island's assembly made known its gratitude to Queen Victoria for this unprecedented voluntary withdrawal by a great power from an overseas possession.

Peace settled on the island in its early years as a province of Greece. Aristocratic tourists converged here, and Empress Elisabeth of Austria liked it so much that she commissioned an elaborate palace, which became the Achilleion.

Though officially neutral during the first three years of World War I, Corfu effectively served as an Allied military and naval base, recalling the role the island had played in previous centuries. In 1916 Corfu gave refuge to the exiled government of Serbia and its troops after they were driven from the mainland. Thousands died from wounds and disease and now lie in Serbian cemeteries on Vídos Island and near Ágios Matthéos.

In 1923 Mussolini gave an order for his fleet to bombard the island in reprisal for the alleged assassination of one of his generals on the Albanian-Greek border. Italian forces occupied Corfu briefly until they were obliged to withdraw under diplomatic pressure (primarily from Great Britain).

The Italians returned as occupiers in World War II. Mussolini issued new currency, renamed streets and signalled his intention to annex the Ionian Islands. However, Italy subsequently capitulated in September 1943.

When the Germans tried to succeed their defeated allies, the Italian troops (who had now switched sides) resisted on Corfu and throughout the Ionians. In the ensuing battles and bombardments, nearly a quarter of Kérkyra Town was destroyed, including the parliament house, academy and municipal theatre. After a year of occupation, German forces evacuated Corfu in October 1944. The British moved in, and peace reigned once more.

Life in the villages changed little in the 20th century

Corfu was largely unaffected by the Greek civil war between communist and royalist partisans that raged on the mainland between 1947 and 1949. Since then, tourism and agriculture – the two economic mainstays of the island – have brought unprecedented prosperity to much of Corfu.

Historical Landmarks

734BC Corinthians found colony of Corcyra.

665BC Corcyra defeats Corinth and gains independence.

229BC–AD337 Romans control Corfu, their first colony in the Adriatic.

337 Roman Empire splits; Corfu becomes part of Byzantine Empire.

562 Ostrogoths destroy ancient capital city and monuments.

933 Corfiots establish new capital and build first fortress.

1080–5 Normans from Sicily repeatedly invade Corfu.

1204 Fall of Constantinople to Fourth Crusade; Venice controls Corfu.

1214–59 Despotate of Epirus takes control of Corfu.

1259–1386 Kings of Sicily, mostly the Angevin dynasty, rule Corfu.

1386 Venetian occupation establishes Corfu as a key port for commercial routes and an important naval base.

1537 Kékyra Town withstands first Turkish siege; countryside sacked.

1576–88 Venice erects great city walls and fortresses at Kérkyra.

1716 Corfiots, Venetians and allies withstand six-week Ottoman seige of Corfu.

1797 Napoleon defeats Venice and claims the Ionian Islands for France.

1799 Russians and Turks defeat French and seize Corfu.

1800–07 'Septinsular Republic' controlled by Russia and Turkey.

1807–14 Russians cede Ionian Islands to the French.

1814–63 Corfu becomes a British protectorate.

1828 Mainland Greece wins independence from Turkey.

1864 Britain gives up protectorate, cedes Ionian Islands to Greece.

1916 Corfu gives refuge to exiled Serbian government.

1941 Corfu surrenders to Italy.

1943 Kérkyra Town badly damaged by German bombardment. Nazis occupy Corfu.

1944 Corfu liberated by the Allies.

1951 Club Mediterranée opens in Ýpsos.

1994 The island hosts European Union Summit.

2002 Greece adopts the euro.

2004 Greece wins Euro 2004 football tournament.

WHERE TO GO

Although Kérkyra Town (Corfu Town) is in many ways the heart and soul of the island, like most capitals it is neither typical nor representative. Unless you are travelling independently or just visiting Corfu on a whistle-stop tour, it is unlikely that you will be staying overnight in Kérkyra Town.

The vast majority of Corfu's visitors are on package tours and invariably stay on the coast at a broad range of accommodation – from cheap-and-cheerful hotels to luxury villas. Most such visitors are simply looking for 'rest and recreation'. Nonetheless, Kérkyra Town acts as a magnet for shoppers, culture vultures, or the merely curious, and it rarely disappoints. Located about halfway down the east coast, it is within striking distance of any spot on the island and thus makes a useful reference point for us to begin our island tour.

We divide our tour of the rest of the island into the following sections:

The South. The long, narrow southern portion of the island is often described (usually by people who haven't been to Corfu) as nothing more than a party zone. This is certainly true of its extremity (Kávos) but is not true when applied to the whole area. The Achilleion Palace is Corfu's most-visited cultural attraction, while the long laid-back beaches of Ágios Geórgios and peaceful fishing villages such as Boúkari provide a sharp contrast to the busy resorts of Benítses, Moraïtika and Mesongí, so popular with British visitors.

North of Kérkyra Town. Immediately north of the capital is the most developed part of the island. Its resorts are mostly hidden from the main road, occupying the large bays and inlets on this stretch of coastline.

The Northeast. Look in any brochure of expensive holiday villas and you will find most are set in the small area between Barbáti and Kassiópi. The Durrells made Kalámi the most famous resort on this stretch, but there are many similar ones nestling in the exquisite tiny coves that make this area 'connoisseur's Corfu'. A short distance inland looms imperious Mt Pandokrátor.

The North and Northwest. While the north coast is well developed and dominated by the resorts of Sidári and Róda, the northwest remains something of a mystery to the majority of visitors. The resorts of Ágios Geórgios and Ágios Stéfanos are very different from their namesakes south and east, respectively. Until recently they have been relatively isolated, but new roads have changed all that. The jewel of the northwest is Paleokastrítsa, boasting one of the most beautiful bays in all of Europe and retaining some charm despite its huge popularity.

The West. Between Érmones and Ágios Górdis, the west is best for beautiful sandy beaches. Until recently it had escaped the attention of large-scale tourism, but development is now encroaching here as it has elsewhere on the island.

An elegant Corfiot

KÉRKYRA TOWN

Kérkyra Town (Corfu Town) is a beguiling place, with a relaxed, old-world elegance that rivals other Mediterranean cities many times its size. Its predominantly Venetian architecture is harmoniously flavoured with French and English Georgian building styles, reflecting the influence of several centuries of foreign occupation. A cosmopolitan nature prevails, especially at night, when Corfiots and visitors stroll along the Liston and rendezvous at the many cafés and restaurants. In early August the atmosphere is very Italian.

Around the Esplanade

The focal point of Kérkyra Town is the **Esplanade** (Spianáda). Families promenade, marching bands parade and festive

Arriving in the Capital

If you are driving into Kérkyra Town, it's best to park as close as possible to one or the other of the two forts; this helps you get your bearings. The two forts effectively mark the eastern and western boundaries of the town centre. From the top of either one, you can quickly appreciate the scale and layout below.

Driving in Kérkyra Town is less stressful than its myriad streets would suggest, thanks to an efficient one-way system. If you cannot park by the Old Fort, you will simply be routed round to the New Fort.

Public buses set down either at San Rocco Square (blue buses) or near the New Fort (green buses). San Rocco Square (Sarókko in Greek) is Corfu's Piccadilly Circus or Times Square, intimidatingly busy at most times of the day. Although it is only a stone's throw away from the tourist centre of Corfu, this is a very 'Greek' part of town, with most shops and businesses catering to locals. Visitors who arrive by coach excursion disembark close to the New Fort and the grassy gardens of the Esplanade.

Do note that our description of the town involves some backtracking and – because things are so close together – a little duplication. Kérkyra Town might be a relatively small place, but it definitely rewards lingering. It is impossible to do the town justice in a single day. You should certainly aim to come here on Tuesday, Thursday or Friday, when the shops open in the evening.

occasions are frequently celebrated on this broad green expanse separating the Old Fort from the rest of town. The area was razed in Venetian times to give a clear field of fire against enemy assault, and it was also used for fairs and jousting tournaments. The French later planted the palms, trees and flower gardens.

On the southern half of the Esplanade is the plain **Ionian Monument**, which celebrates the island's union with Greece in 1864. It is surrounded by marble reliefs displaying the symbols of the seven Ionian Islands, which are known as the Eptánisa in Greek. Nearby is the Victorian bandstand (where Sunday concerts are held in summer) and the Maitland Rotunda, dedicated to the first British high commissioner. At the far end is the statue of Greece's first president (1827–31) and

That's Cricket

Kérkyra Town cricket pitch is one of the most unusual sportsgrounds in the world. Kim Hughes, the Australian captain during the early 1980s, once hit a mighty six right over the gardens and into the moat of the Old Fort here.

The mixed cultural heritage of the island can be heard in the cricketing language. '*Play*' is the Corfiot name for cricket. But, perhaps because of the long association with the Venetians, more than one term used during play has been lifted from Italian. So when a 'long hop' becomes *primo salto* and cricket stumps are *xýla* ('woods' in Greek), the English might feel at a loss in their own game. Still, when the former England captain David Gower was asked where he had enjoyed playing the most, his immediate reply was: 'It has to be Corfu'.

Today the cricket pitch in Kérkyra Town is mainly used by the island's under-18 and under-14 youth teams, since the size of the pitch was reduced to make room for a car park. Adult matches take place in the new cricket ground at Gouvia Marina.

Corfu's greatest son, Ioánnis Kapodístrias.

The Esplanade's most famous landmark is the cricket pitch dominating its northern half. Corfu adopted this sport during British rule, and enthusiastic local teams keep the tradition alive with matches during the season.

The Maitland Rotunda

Across the north side of the Esplanade stands the imposing **Palace of St Michael and St George**, erected between 1818 and 1823 by Maltese masons as the residence for the British high commissioners, with a neoclassical façade of 32 Doric columns linking triumphal arches. It also housed the Ionian senate. When the British left, Greek royalty used it as a summer residence. The bronze toga-clad figure who stands above a lily pond in front of the palace is Sir Frederick Adam, Britain's second high commissioner. The pool and its water spouts are there to remind people that Adam was the first to ensure Kérkyra Town a reliable water supply, with an aqueduct system still in use today.

The palace's state rooms now house the **Museum of Asiatic Art** (open Tues–Sun 8.30am–3pm; entrance fee). Its collection of over 11,000 Asian artefacts is one of the most comprehensive of its kind in the world. Ancient pieces include funerary statuary and bowls, pottery and ceramics from various Chinese dynasties and other Asian origins – Chou ritual bronzes, Ming Buddhas, ancient Cambodian stone heads, decorative dishware, intricate screens, silks and ivory. The west wing contains Japanese woodblock prints, miniature art, lacquer ware, tea ceremony utensils, theatre masks and Samurai weapons and armour.

The elegant Liston façade, inspired by the Rue de Rivoli in Paris

Around the back of the palace (on the Old Fort side), set in lovely gardens, is the lesser-known **Municipal Art Gallery** (open daily 8.30am–3pm; entrance fee). It is a modest collection comprising mostly 19th- and 20th-century works by Corfiot artists. Look for the *Assassination of Kapodístrias* in Room 2, portraying the murder of the island's most famous native son, as well as the charming, French-inspired *Night in Corfu* in Room 5, which shows that even in 1913 the Liston was the place to be. Room 3 contains several fine Italian-influenced religious paintings of the 16th and 17th centuries. After browsing the pictures, enjoy a coffee in the delightful setting of the adjacent Art Gallery Café.

On the opposite side of the palace, just across the street, visit the pretty yellow building with an arcaded façade, and an outside staircase leading up to a small loggia. This is home to the **Corfu Reading Society**, the oldest cultural institution in modern Greece, founded in 1836. Here on weekday mornings (closed in August) you can browse the history of the Ionian Islands in an archived collection of photographs, books, manuscripts and other documents.

The elegant arcades of the **Liston** border the west side of the Esplanade. Inspired by the Rue de Rivoli in Paris, it was built by the French in 1807. Its name comes from the 'list' of noble families who were the only ones permitted to walk here. These days everyone gathers at the many cafés and bars under the arches or beneath the trees along the green. During the evening this pedestrian-only street is transformed into a bustling promenade of Corfiots and visitors alike, from dapper elderly men to smartly dressed families.

Stroll down the length of **Kapodistríou Street**, which runs from behind the Liston to the southern end of the green. It is lined with handsome homes, most of which were built by the Venetian-era aristocracy, and several picturesque streets lead off here into town. Moustoxýdi Street, for example, used to be an important thoroughfare and was also the setting for jousting displays during Carnival, with the judges seated on the balcony above the ornate portico of the Ricchi mansion. At the very end of Kapodistríou, on Akadimías Street, looms the pink façade of the former Ionian Academy, founded in 1824 by Lord Guilford as the first modern Greek university. Like much of the surrounding area, it has been completely rebuilt after suffering destruction in the heavy bombing of 1943, and today appropriately is used by the University of the Ionian.

Kérkyra's busy shopping district

Dousmáni Street cuts across the Esplanade to the Old Fort. Here you will find a string of colourful 19th-century horse-cabs *(carrozzi),* which will take you on a ride around Kérkyra Town. Be sure to agree on the fare before you set out.

The Old Fort (Paleó Froúrio)

Kérkyra Town grew up on the eastern peninsula around the **Old Fort** (Paleó Froúrio; open daily 8.30am–3pm, possibly 7pm in summer; entrance fee), which was erected for protection from barbarian raiders in the 10th century. The two peaks of the promontory on which it stands were the source of the name Corfu, a corruption of *koryfí* (summit in Greek).

The Old Fort and its marina

A statue of Count Schulenburg, the German mercenary who led the Corfiot defence against the Turkish attack of 1716, stands outside the entrance to the Old Fort, one of the many fortifications added by the Venetians to the older Byzantine citadel on the eastern peak. Its defensive moat, the Contrafossa, is lined with small fishing boats and utility sheds, making for a very picturesque and peaceful scene. In turbulent times in the past, the bridge could be raised, cutting off all access to the fort.

The Venetian seat of government was based here until it was destroyed by the

British, who built barracks and a military hospital. The fort was then used by the Greek army until 1979. Restoration has been going on ever since, with the most recent additions being an excellent, small Byzantine museum (admission included in the fort ticket) containing bird mosaics from the Iovianós Basilica at Paleópolis, plus late Byzantine frescoes.

You can save a considerable amount on site admissions by buying a combined ticket for €8. This allows entry to the Archaeological Museum, the Museum of Asiatic Art, the Byzantine Museum and the Old Fort, over a period of a few days.

Once you are inside the fort complex, a path to the right leads to the neoclassical garrison church of **St George**, built by the British in 1840 as an Anglican chapel and restored after damage during World War II. Now converted to a Greek Orthodox church, it has a fine stone iconostasis and icons but, thanks to its origins, is plain and box-like inside, with no columns or aisles.

Come back toward the entrance, where a stone path leads past a Venetian clocktower up to the lighthouse on the higher peak. The steep climb is well worth it for the spectacular panorama of Kérkyra Town, the harbour, the airport and Mt Pandokrátor to the north.

From the Liston to the New Fort

From the northern end of the Liston, walk along Kapodistríou Street, passing the Corfu Reading Society, and enter Arseníou Street. Look back to your right for a fine view of the Old Fort and its marina. Immediately below is a small promontory, with a clutch of restaurants, cafés and a swimming area.

The green, densely forested islet just offshore is **Vídos Island**, today a bird sanctuary but once the base for Ottoman attacks in 1537 and 1716. Its fortifications were destroyed when the British left the island in 1864, and it subsequently became a prison; the ruins are now a minor attraction. The island served as a refugee camp for around 150,000 Serbian soldiers during World War I. Sadly, some 30,000 of them died from influenza and other diseases caused by unsanitary living conditions; a mausoleum is dedicated to them. Boats regularly shuttle between the island and the Old Port.

A short way along Arseníou Street, a flight of steps leads to the excellent **Byzantine Museum**, housed in the 15th-century Basilica of Panagía Andivouniótissa (off Arseníou Street; open Tues–Sun 8.30am–3pm; entrance fee). The single-aisle, timber-roofed church is one of the oldest and richest on the island, constructed in the traditional Corfiot manner with a vestibule around three sides. In the museum there is an impressive array of icons from the 15th to 19th centuries.

The Byzantine Museum occupies a 15th-century basilica

Around the corner, the imposing profile of the **New Fort** (open daily 9am–9pm; entrance fee) heaves into view beyond the Old Port. The New Fort (also known as the Fort of San Marco) was built by the Venetians between 1572 and 1645, shortly after the second of two major Turkish sieges. You can see the Venetian emblem – the winged lion of St

The New Fort

Mark – in stone relief above the massive gates. The French, and later the British, completed the fortifications. The town's fruit and vegetable market is now held in the dry moat on the western side. A series of secret tunnels is said to connect the new and old fortresses (and even Vídos Island). Occasionally, temporary exhibitions or concerts are held inside the walls, but the finest sight is the superb view of Kérkyra Town and the far coast.

On the northern edge of Kérkyra Town's centre – on the waterfront west of the New Fort, towards the New Port – is a lively nightlife strip with several clubs, bars and music venues. These are particularly busy in the first half of August, when young Italian holidaymakers make merry.

The Commercial Centre

The centre of town starts roughly where I. Theotóki Street meets M. Theotóki Street (via Evangelistrías). Do note the first initials of these streets – there are several thoroughfares named after members of this long-established, illustrious Corfiot family. Off M. Theotóki are five parallel shopping streets, all of which run into Kapodistríou: they are Voul-

The belltower of Ágios Spyrídon

gáreos, Agíon Pándon, Sevastianou, N. Theotóki and Agíou Spyrídonos.

Nikifórou Theotóki is the commercial centre's 'High Street', leading all the way from the Old Port to Kapodistríou. Its main square is Platía Iróon Kypriakón Agonistón (Square of the Cypriot Fighters); however, because it backs onto St Spyridon's Church, it is better known as Platía Agiou Spyrídonas (St Spyridon's Square). In the centre of the square stands a statue of Corfiot politician Georgios Theotóki (1843–1916).

On the western side of the square stands the island's oldest bank, the Ionian, opened in 1839. It is home to the **Paper Money Museum** (open summer Mon–Fri 10am–2pm; free), featuring an extensive display ranging from early Ionian banknotes to world currency. More interesting than it sounds, this impressive collection illustrates all the stages in designing, printing and releasing notes for circulation. Adding to the confusion, the bank has given the square yet another unofficial name: Platía Ionikí.

Across from the bank stands the **Faneroméni** church, also called Our Lady of the Foreigners (Panagía tón Xénon) because it was inhabited by refugees from the mainland during the time of the Ottoman occupation of Greece. Erected in 1689, it is lavishly decorated with gilded wood, a beautifully painted ceiling and icons by Cretan painters. Opposite is a simpler church, **St John the Baptist** (Ágios

Ioánnis o Pródromos). Built in 1520, it was formerly Corfu's cathedral and also contains important Cretan icons.

The red-domed belltower of the church of **Ágios Spyrí-donos**, the tallest on the island, rises north of the square. It was founded in 1590 to house the mummified body of Corfu's beloved saint, who lies in an ornate silver coffin in a chapel to the right of the altar. On certain days the casket is opened, and on special feast days the saint is paraded upright through town. His shrunken face can be seen through a glass panel, and his slippered feet are exposed for the faithful to kiss. With all the rich Venetian oil lamps swinging above the casket (plus the chandeliers and the

---

St Spyrídon

Corfiots pray to him, swear by him, name their sons after him and honour him with a remarkable passion. He is the island's beloved patron saint, yet he wasn't even born on Corfu.

Spyrídon was a village shepherd on the distant island of Cyprus. He became a monk, then a bishop, and was noted for his devoutness and ability to effect minor miracles. After his death in AD350, a sweet odour wafted from his grave; his body was exhumed and found to be perfectly preserved. The saint's remains were taken to Constantinople but were smuggled out (with those of St Theodora Augusta) before the Turkish occupation in 1453. Unceremoniously wrapped in a sack of straw strapped to a mule, the remains arrived in Corfu in 1456. In time, Spyrídon became the object of enthusiastic veneration.

To honour his miracles, his casket is paraded through Kérkyra Town in colourful processions on Orthodox Palm Sunday, Easter Saturday, 11 August, and the first Sunday in November. St Spyrídon has reputedly saved the island four times: twice from the plague, once from famine, and once (in 1716) from the Turks. Small wonder that most Corfiot men are named Spyros.

The marble-clad Town Hall stands in Platía Nikifórou Theotóki

candelabra), this modest, dimly lit church is said to have the greatest amount of silver of any Greek church outside the island of Tínos. Frescoes on the ceiling depict the saint's miracles.

Leave the church by the front entrance, on Agíou Spyrídonos Street. Go to the left to meet Filarmonikís Street. Here you can turn right to explore the Old Town. Or you can turn left to reach M. Theotóki Street to see more of the shopping district. (If you have time do both, see the Old Town first and then retrace your steps.)

Follow M. Theotóki Street to the corner of Voulgáreos Street, behind which is **Platía Nikifórou Theotóki**, once the main square of the Old Town. It too has another name: Platía Dhimarkhíou (Town Hall Square). At the lowest part of the square sits the **Town Hall**, one of Corfu's most decorative buildings. Built by the Venetians in 1663 out of white marble from the eastern slopes of Mt Pandokrátor, its original single-storey loggia served as a meeting place for the nobility. It was converted into a theatre in 1720, and later a second storey was added. It became the Town Hall in 1903. The façade is adorned with carved masks and medallions. On the eastern wall there is a bust of Francesco Morosini, the Venetian commander who defeated the Ottomans at Athens in 1687.

Handsome steps and flower-decked terraces ascend above the square, past restaurants and some smart shops. The stately building at the top was originally the Catholic archbishop's palace. It was subsequently converted into the Law Courts, and now it is home to the Bank of Greece.

The Old Town

The **Old Town** is the fascinating maze of narrow streets, steep stairways and arched alleys squeezed into the northeast quadrant of Kérkyra Town, between the Old Fort and the Old Port. It has been described as Greece's largest 'living medieval town'. As you wander along the flagstone streets, peeking into open doorways, you might feel that this traffic-free, tall-walled quarter is like a miniature Venice – minus the canals, of course. The northernmost part has even retained its Venetian name, **Campiello**.

In the heart of the Campiello

In Venetian times, the area between the old and new forts was surrounded by city walls (torn down during the 19th century). As Corfiots weren't permitted to live outside the walls, the only direction in which they could expand their living quarters was upwards, producing the district's unusually high buildings. And, just as in the less-touristy parts of Venice, much of the Old Town's appeal is in its residential atmosphere, with laundry strung across alleyways, old women on stools weaving or keeping an eye on babies, and cats snoozing in tiny sun-splashed squares. The only 'sight' is the charming 17th-century **Venetian Well** on the Campiello's Platía Kremastí, where one of the city's best restaurants sets out its tables.

There are many ways of entering the Campiello, and it's an excellent place to simply wander at will. However, here is one way to find the Venetian Well from the landmark church of St Spyrídon: outside the church (front entrance), turn left into Ágios Spyrídon Street and, at the end, turn right into Filarmonikís, then left again into Filellínon, a narrow passageway lined with shops. The maze-like streets that make up the heart of the Campiello will be to your right. As you emerge from Filellínon, turn right into Agías Theodóras. Look for a short flight of steps on the left, which lead to Platía Kremastí.

By retracing your route along Agías Theodóras, you'll reach Corfu's **Orthodox Cathedral**, built in 1577 and dedicated to St Theodora, the island's second-most-revered saint (after Spyrídon). Her headless body, which was spirited out of Constantinople (along with Spyrídon's), lies in a silver reliquary to the right of the altar screen. There is a serene, slightly Eastern beauty to this small church. Broad flights of steps lead down to the harbour, and Corfiots often momentarily pause here to light a candle before or after embarking on a sea journey.

Archaeological Treasures

The island's prime collection of antiquities is a five-minute walk south of the Old Fort, along the coastal road past the marina. A signpost just after the Corfu Palace Hotel

The massive Gorgon pediment in the Archaeological Museum

announces the **Archaeological Museum** (5 Vraïla Street; open Tues–Sun 8.30am–3pm; entrance fee). ◄

This pleasantly airy, modern museum houses two of the finest works of antiquity ever found. The star attraction, the **Gorgon pediment**, comes from the Temple of Artemis (6th-century BC) at ancient Corcyra. It derives its name from the ferocious, sculpted Medusa (the most infamous of the three snake-haired gorgons), shown here with wings at her back, winged sandals, and serpents at her waist. She is flanked by her offspring, born from her dying blood: Pegasus, the winged horse, and the hero Khrysaor. Beside her stand two alert lion-panthers waiting to obey the commands of this monster who, according to the myth, turned anyone who met her gaze to stone. The pediment was discovered in 1912 at Paleópolis and is Greece's oldest existing monumental sculpture. What makes it particularly fearsome are the glazed, bulging eyes and the sheer scale: she stands some 3m (10ft) tall.

The verdant tranquillity of the British Cemetery

Not so colossal – but almost as important in archæological terms – is the Archaic lion in the adjoining room. This remarkable sculpture, dating from the same period as the Gorgon pediment, was found near the Tomb of Menekrates in 1843 and is thought to have graced the grave of a warrior during Corcyra's struggle for independence from Corinth. The lion was chiselled by an unknown Corinthian artist and is considered one of the most beautiful ancient animal sculptures.

Among the museum's other treasures, which include pottery, coins, bronze statuettes, figurines and Neolithic artefacts, is the series of small statues depicting the goddess Artemis in her different guises as huntress, protector and guardian of the hearth. They are thought to have been produced for local worshippers in what might have been Corfu's first souvenir shop.

A five-minute walk south of the museum brings you to another treat for archaeology enthusiasts. The **Tomb of Menekrates** lies one block inland from the monument to Sir

Howard Douglas, another high commissioner, at the intersection of the coastal road and Alexándras Avenue. This circular stone cenotaph with a conical roof was a tribute to Menekrates, a mercenary who fought on the mainland in Corcyra's interests. It dates from about 600BC.

As you head back toward the centre of town along Maraslí Street, it is a five-minute walk to the serenely beautiful **British Cemetery**, which retains special significance for a large number of British and Commonwealth visitors. Among the tall cypress trees and meticulously kept flowers and shrubbery (beautiful wild flowers, even orchids, also grow here) lie graves that date back to the start of Britain's protectorate. There are graves of British servicemen from the two world wars as well. The circular wall south of the cemetery encloses the penitentiary. Built by the British, it was once the most modern penal institute in Europe, with individual cells for inmates. It is still in use today, though ironically it now has one of the worst reputations in Greece.

Southern Suburbs

To explore this part of Corfu you will need transport, or be willing to hop on and off blue city buses marked 'KANONI'. Head south along the coastal road for about 2km (a mile or so) and turn inland (right) to the Byzantine **Church of Ágii Iásonas and Sosípatros**. Built of limestone, brick and tile, this is one of only two surviving Byzantine churches on the island. It is dedicated to saints Jason and Sosípatros, the evangelists credited with bringing Christianity to Corfu in the 2nd century. The present church dates back to the 12th century, though earlier versions stood here during Corfu's Byzantine period (337–1204). The black marble columns in the vestibule and a number of the large blocks used for the walls are thought to be from Classical buildings. The church has undergone major renovation work and is rarely open.

Near the roundabout at Análipsi, a steep path leads down to Kardáki Spring. The water that flows from the mouth of a stone lion – cool in the summer and warm in the winter – is reputed never to dry up. Legend has it that anyone who drinks from the spring is destined to return to Corfu.

Further along the road to Kanóni stands the entrance to the villa and gardens of **Mon Repos**. Built in 1831 by High Commissioner Frederick Adam as a summer residence, it later became the property of the Greek royal family. (Prince Philip, the Duke of Edinburgh, was born here in 1921.) In recent years Mon Repos was the subject of an ownership dispute between ex-king Constantine and the government, which was only resolved in 1996. Since then the villa has been restored and now contains the Museum of Paleópolis (open Tues–Sun 8.30am–3pm; entrance fee). There are period furnishings from Adams' time, and fascinating artefacts and exhibits depicting life in ancient Corcyra, including a scale model of the town and Paleópolis peninsula. Paths wind along the wooded promontory, past an old chapel with vine-covered arbours, up to a scenic view of the shore below. Follow the 'ancient temple' signs for a 15-minute walk to the remains of a small Doric temple dating from 500BC.

Ancient Corcyra

Opposite the Mon Repos gate lie the commanding ruins of **Agía Kérkyra**. This 5th-century basilica is the oldest church on the island, constructed from remnants of far older pagan temples that once stood on the site. It was ruined by invaders, rebuilt several times in the ensuing centuries, then destroyed again in World War II.

During the 8th century BC, the original Corinthian city of Corcyra sprawled over much of the area between Mon

Repos and Kanóni, now called **Paleópolis**. You'll see archaeological digs in progress (no entry). A narrow road behind the dig site opposite the basilica leads to the hamlet of Análipsi, thought to be the acropolis of the ancient city of Corcyra. From the church at the top of the hill there is a superb view of the Mon Repos grounds.

Along the road toward Kanóni, you'll see a side road marked 'Stratía'. Here are the ruins of the **Temple of Artemis**, where the gorgon in the Archaeological Museum was excavated. Next door is the Convent of Agía Theodóra. Further along the road stands one of the sections of the wall of ancient Corcyra, dating from the 5th century BC.

Kanóni

Generations of earlier visitors knew **Kanóni** as a tranquil green peninsula, a pleasant walk or carriage ride south of the

The monastery of Panagía Vlahernón off the Kanóni Peninsula

capital. Popular with Corfiots, it also used to attract large groups of British residents, who came to admire the most famous view on the island: the two islets resting peacefully in the Halikopoúlou lagoon.

Times have changed. New hotels and blocks of flats have disfigured the landscape. The motivation for building hotels and residences here is unclear, as many of their views are of the shallow and murky lagoon and the adjacent international airport runway, complete with thunderous sound effects. In fact, it might be said that Kanóni has come full circle: its name derives from the gun battery that the French installed on the hillside here in 1798. Nevertheless, the delightful picture-postcard **view** of the islets and the coastal scenery beyond them remains intact, attracting an endless stream of tour buses to Kanóni. A far nicer way to arrive is on the boats that run hourly from Kérkyra Town.

Contrary to popular belief, the islet in the foreground – linked to the mainland by a causeway – is not Mouse Island but **Vlahérna**, which is home to a pretty, tiny, white convent (Panagía Vlahernón). **Mouse Island** (or Pondikonísi) lies a three-minute boat trip away. There, an even smaller 13th-century chapel lies hidden beneath the cypress trees, though in reality it is of little interest and hardly worth the journey. Mouse Island is another contender for the site of the mythical Phaeacian ship turned to stone *(see page 12)*.

A pair of café-restaurants on the hill provide a relaxing terrace from which to enjoy the magnificent view. A pedestrian causeway below leads across the lagoon to Pérama.

The Achilleion Palace
Described by the British writer Lawrence Durrell as 'a monstrous building' and by the American Henry Miller as 'the worst piece of gimcrackery I have ever laid eyes on', the
► **Achilleion (Achíllio) Palace** (open daily 9am–3.30pm, June–

Corfu's most popular tourist sight: the 'monstrous' Achilleion Palace

Aug 8am–7pm; entrance fee) is one of the most popular sights on the island, and usually teeming with tour coaches. Used as a backdrop in the James Bond film *For Your Eyes Only*, the palace is situated some 10km (6 miles) south of Kérkyra Town.

A romantic past as an imperial hideaway is a large part of the palace's attraction. The beautiful Empress Elisabeth of Austria (known as Princess Sisi) fell in love with this site on a visit to the island in the 1860s. Two decades later – desperately unhappy, stifled by the pomp of Vienna and stricken by the death of her only son – she looked back with longing to Corfu. In 1890 she bought this land and commissioned the building of a palace that would be worthy of her idol, the Greek hero Achilles. The result, built in the neoclassical style of the late 19th century, was criticised as being tasteless and ostentatious.

The empress nonetheless spent as much time as she possibly could at the Achilleion, in utmost seclusion in the spring and autumn of each year. But poor Sisi had only a few years to enjoy her palace. Her tragic life came to a premature end in 1898 when, during a visit to Switzerland, she was mortally stabbed by an Italian anarchist.

In 1907 Kaiser Wilhelm II of Germany acquired the palace, deeming it a suitable base from which to pursue his archaeological hobby. He invited dignitaries from all over Europe to attend parties and concerts here. Because most arrived by boat, he built a bridge at the seashore that crossed the coastal road directly to his palace. Only the ruins of the bridge, ironically destroyed by the German army in 1943, remain today. The Kaiser also installed an awesome 4.5-ton bronze *Victorious Achilles,* which looms some 11.5m (38ft) high at the far end of the gardens.

Kaiser Wilhelm's mighty Achilles

The Achilleion was used as a military hospital in World War I. It subsequently became the property of the Greek government, and from 1962 to 1983 its opulent upper floors were converted into a casino. In the 1990s, after renovation and the removal of its casino, the palace was opened to the public, though only half a dozen ground-floor rooms are visitable.

The Achilleion is adorned both inside and out with a flurry of pseudo-Classical statues, with Greek gods, goddesses and heroes filling every corner. Those surrounding the Peristyle of the

Muses, outside the palace, are copies of the ones in Rome's Villa Borghese gardens. Do make sure to peer through the window here to see the giant painting *The Triumph of Achilles* by Franz Matz. (It is on the first floor of the palace, which is closed to the public.) Our hero is shown in brutal, vengeful form dragging the body of Hector behind his chariot around the walls of Troy as a reprisal for the killing of Achilles' friend Patroclus.

> Among all the statues scattered about the grounds, only one is considered by experts to have any artistic merit: the dramatic *Dying Achilles*, by German sculptor Ernst Herter.

Inside, the ground-floor rooms house a small chapel and the original furnishings and memorabilia of the empress and the Kaiser. One unusual attraction is the adjustable saddle on which Wilhelm used to sit while writing at his desk.

The extensive grounds are perhaps the true highlight of the Achilleion. The manicured hilltop gardens are a real pleasure, with magnificent sweeping views over the island.

THE SOUTH

Benítses, some 12km (7½ miles) south of the capital, used to be the island's nonstop party town, but no longer. It now attracts a much quieter clientele. The town is set to revamp its image with the opening of a smart new marina opposite the main square in 2006, with new restaurants and bars to cater for the yachting crowd.

Arriving from the north, the first thing you will see in Benítses is the **Shell Museum** (open daily 10am–8pm; entrance fee). This impressive exhibition of seashells, corals, fossils, starfish and sponges was collected throughout the world by a Corfiot. It is one of the best private shell collections in Europe. The many specimens on display range from huge clamshells to tiny delicate cowries, fearsome shark's jaws, spiny crustacean skeletons and stuffed pufferfish.

It is thought that Benítses might have been a holiday centre as far back as Roman times. Behind the harbour square stand the meagre remains of what was once a Roman bathhouse, together with some floor mosaics. This northern end of town, near the old harbour, has a very Greek atmosphere, with pretty cottages that retain the character of the original fishing village. The emerald valley at the western edge of town is crisscrossed with footpaths in an unexpected wilderness.

Moraïtika and Mesongí

The busy coastal road continues south as far as the twin resorts of Moraïtika and Mesongí, 20km (12½ miles) from Kérkyra Town. They lie at the mouth of – and are divided by – the Mesongí river. This is an attractive spot, with fishing and pleasure boats moored alongside the riverfront.

Moraïtika is the busier and livelier of the two villages. Its older section is set on a hill just off the main road and marked by a red-and-yellow campanile. There is no tourist develop-

---

The Venerable Olive

Almost everyone on Corfu owns a few olive trees. In Venetian times, peasants were paid a bonus for each tree they planted, and by the 17th century a family's wealth was determined by the number of trees it owned. Today there are said to be 3.5 million on the island.

According to legend, St Spyrídon appeared in an olive grove and proclaimed that cutting or beating the trees was cruel. As a result, Corfiots neither prune the branches nor pick the fruit. Instead, they let the olives fall to the ground naturally, where huge nets are spread to catch them. Trees bear fruit only every other year and might take 12 years to yield a first crop.

ment up here, just an attractive taverna or two providing a nice antidote to the seaside resort below. Like Moraïtika, **Mesongí** features an increasing amount of development, now spreading back from the long but very narrow beaches. Behind the beach, Mesongí has some of Corfu's oldest olive groves, planted by the Venetians over 500 years ago. The hills are perfect for walking.

Olive groves near Mesongí

From here the main road south curves inland and reaches a T-junction at Áno Mesongí. The route north takes you inland through the pastoral scenery of the Mesongí river valley before ascending the slopes of Corfu's second-tallest mountain, the 576-m (1,889-ft) Ágii Déka ('Ten Saints'). From **Ágii Déka** village there is a spectacular view out to sea, overlooking Benítses and the distant Kanóni Peninsula.

An alternative route to the southern tip of the island is not to turn inland but to follow the minor road that runs along the coast southward from Mesongí. Along this peaceful, tree-shaded shore are small seafood tavernas and narrow, pebbly beaches where you can soak up the tranquil bay view. It's a far cry from the busy international resorts you have just passed. This pretty stretch ends at the small fishing village of **Boúkari**. But if you would like a little more of the same, head inland, then seaward again, either to the little fishing village of Nótos or to Petríti, another quiet spot where fresh fish is a speciality.

Directly opposite here, on Corfu's southwest coast, lies the island's longest sandy beach, nicknamed 'Golden Sands'. To reach it from Boúkari, return to the main road where the old monastery at Argyrádes sports a striking Venetian belfry. Head east for 2km (1¼ miles) and at Marathiás village a makeshift sign points down to the right, to 'THE BEACH'. This refers to a beach known as **Agía Varvára**, Marathiá or Maltás (or Santa Barbara on some maps). Whatever the name, it is an attractive broad stretch of soft golden sand, which continues north through Ágios Geórgios all the way to Lake Korissíon.

To get to the busy resort of **Ágios Geórgios south**, head back north and then turn left shortly after Argyrádes. The turn-off leads to the busiest part of the place, with development sprawling for about 2km (a mile or so) along the frontage road. However, once away from the resort the beach remains very attractive, with golden sand backed by impressive cliffs.

The northernmost part of the beach is **Íssos**, which borders the lagoon of **Korissíon**. To get there you have to return to

Agía Varvára is part of the longest sandy beach on all Corfu

the main road, head north and turn left at Línia. Lake Koríssíon is a protected area, thus off limits for swimming or boating, but bird-watchers will find plenty to observe here, particularly in spring and autumn. The scenery at Íssos is quite wild, with tall dunes providing shelter for nudists, and large wind-carved rocks giving a lunar-like landscape. This was a setting for a chase scene in the James Bond film *For Your Eyes Only*. Windsurfing conditions here are excellent, and a small school operates locally.

There is little of interest southeast of Marathiás other than a few secluded beaches. This is olive, orchard and vegetable country as well as the island's principal wine-producing region. **Lefkímmi** is the hub of this working agricultural region, bypassed by a very fast road that goes all the way to the southern tip of the island.

Kávos

Kávos is the end of the road, the last resort – in just about every respect. To Corfiots, the very name brings a shake of the head and a 'tsk tsk' of disapproval. Development has mushroomed since the late 1980s, with a profusion of apartments, hotels and scores of nightspots and music bars flourishing incongruously on this remote tip of the island. Young booze-fuelled revellers flock here in July and August, earning the resort a well-deserved reputation for being the rowdiest on the island. That said, the soft sandy beach that extends for 3km (nearly 2 miles) shelves gently and is popular with families earlier in the season.

There's a variety of water sports available here, as well as bungee-jumping from two towers, and direct boat excursions to Paxí, Párga and Sývota (the latter two on the Greek mainland). A walk through peaceful countryside leads to Cape Asprókavos, the island's southernmost tip, and the monastery of Panagía Arkoudílas, overlooking another superb beach.

NORTH OF KÉRKYRA TOWN

The former fishing villages north of Kérkyra Town are now home to some of the island's liveliest and most popular resorts. The villages of Kondókali and Gouviá lie within a sheltered lagoon about 8km (5 miles) north of the capital. They are set back from the busy main highway and linked by a small road, with side tracks leading to sand and pebble beaches and a large marina.

Gouviá, named after the bay on which it stands, is the more developed of the two villages, with a narrow, compacted sand beach dominated by large hotels. One section is even fronted with concrete so that the sea (shallow and still at this point) looks more like a municipal boating pond than the Ionian. Across the pretty bay you can see the little church of Ypapandí (Candlemas), which juts out on a stone spit rather like the famous 'Mouse Island' vista. Beyond is the island of Lazarétto, which formerly housed a quarantine station.

The extensive harbour of Gouviá has become a private international marina lined with expensive yachts. It was once a Venetian naval base and the skeletal arches of an old Venetian arsenal and shipyard survive at the end of Gouviá's beach. The marina entrance is easily reached from Kondókali. Its gate is manned by a guard but it is open to the public.

On the beach at Dassiá

The resort of **Dassiá** ('forest') is backed by dense olive groves lying between the main road and the sea. There is no central village, just a long string of restaurants, shops and bars along a very busy main road. However, the beach is tucked away down side roads. It is long and narrow, made up of compacted sand and pebbles, and often crowded. There are numerous clubs providing water skiing, jet skiing and parasailing from the long piers jutting out into the bay. The continual stream of colourful parachutes launching off jetties against the blue sky – with the verdant olive groves and mountains in the background – is a fine sight.

To escape the hustle and bustle, wander inland on an uphill journey past quiet villas and olive groves to

Fishing boats in Ýpsos harbour

Káto Korakiána. Here, set in the grounds of an old Venetian villa (the Kastello Mansion), is the **National Gallery and Alexandros Soutzos Museum Annex of Corfu** (open Mon–Wed 10am–2pm and Mon, Wed and Fri 6–9pm; free), which exhibits various works on loan from the Greek National Art Gallery.

The twin resorts of **Ýpsos** and **Pyrgí** are situated on a wide, beautiful bay about 15km (9½ miles) north of Kérkyra Town. Together they have been dubbed 'the Golden Mile' by the armies of young, largely British singles who tend to congregate in the discos and bars of this area in high season. The long, narrow beach that curves around the bay is a mixture of sand and shingle and offers excellent water-sports facilities.

In times past, Ýpsos Bay was a target for Turkish raiders. It is said that the name *Ýpsos,* meaning 'heights', was a ruse to dissuade the Turks from mounting an attack. *Pyrgí,* meaning 'tower', probably derives from watchtowers built to warn of imminent raids. The resorts themselves are recent creations, developing around resettlements of villagers from Ágios Márkos whose homes were destroyed in landslides during the 1950s. Ýpsos at least has retained its fishing fleet, tucked away in an attractive little harbour behind the road as you enter from the south.

The tranquil old village of **Ágios Márkos** (St Mark), signposted just outside Pyrgí, is worth a detour for its glorious views of the coastline, and its two churches. At the top of the village is the 16th-century Church of Christ Pandokrátor, with fresco-covered walls. Lower down, the 11th-century Ágios Merkoúrios, also with ancient frescoes, is Corfu's oldest Byzantine church (the only other one to be found on the island is the Church of Ágii Iásonas and Sosípatros, in Kérkyra Town). Both churches are kept locked; the priest, who lives in Pyrgí by the health clinic, keeps the key.

Icon at the monastery of Ypsiloú Pandokrátora

Mt Pandokrátor

Just beyond the Ágios Márkos turn-off, a road leads to the top of **Mt Pandokrátor** (911m/2,824ft). Around a series of corkscrew bends you'll be greeted by stupendous views over Ýpsos Bay. Just below the colourful village of Spartýlas, the road broadens out into a rolling landscape of fruit trees, fields and vineyards where some of Corfu's finest wine is produced. At Strinýlas there is an inviting bar-restaurant beneath a large elm tree. From this point, continue following the signs to Mt Pandokrátor

It is also possible to get to the top of Mt Pandokrátor from the northeastern part of the island *(see page 62)*. A good tour choice is to go up one side and come down the other.

In the past the summit could be reached only by hiking along a somewhat treacherous gravel track. Today you can drive all the way to the top, but parking space at the summit is limited. If it is busy, park and walk up the last hundred meters. On a clear day you will be rewarded with unbeatable views: the entire sickle outline of Corfu and, over the narrow channel, a glimpse of Albania. To the south, in the blue Ionian, lie the islands of Paxí and distant Lefkáda.

The mountaintop monastery of **Ypsiloú Pandokrátora** (open Apr–Oct 7am–12.30pm and 2.30pm–8pm; free), which shares the summit with an ugly antenna complex, was constructed during the 17th century on the site of an earlier church that had been built by neighbouring villagers in 1347. It has been restored in recent years and is a charming, dark, peaceful haven with many ancient frescoes and icons.

THE NORTHEAST

The dramatic beauty of northeastern Corfu begins above Ýpsos Bay and ends near Kassiópi, a lovely drive over a winding, narrow but paved road stretching some 20km (12½ miles). The road climbs sharply into the steep green slopes that guard the coast, offering tantalising glimpses of the sea below. There are several viewing points along this cliffside road, but most of the shore is hidden and often accessible only by narrow, steep tracks that plunge alarmingly. Some beaches can be reached only on foot. The best way to explore is by boat, which can be

Relaxing on Nisáki's tiny beach

arranged from most jetties. It is worth noting that all the beaches from Ýpsos to Kassiópi are of the pebble variety. Long-range, picture-perfect views often make these white-pebble beaches look like the white sands of the Caribbean, but this is not the case. Nonetheless, swimming is excellent at nearly all the beaches along this coast.

The transition from the commercialised resorts south of Ýpsos Bay to the small and relatively less-developed coves of the northeast peninsula comes at **Barbáti**. There is no steep track to negotiate here, just a gentle slope leading down to sea level, where olive groves shelter a long, pebbly and popular beach with all the usual water sports. The mountains rise steeply behind the beach, making an attractive backdrop. There is some music from beachside and roadside bars, but the atmosphere of Barbáti is very different from that of its southern neighbours.

The next resort along the cliffside road is **Nisáki**, reached by a two-bend drive from the main road. The water here is a crystal-clear medley of greens and blues, though there is hardly room to spread your towel on its tiny pebble beach. It is undoubtedly a lovely spot, with two attractive tavernas, a cluster of shops and accommodation, but you will have to get here early (or late) to stake a beach claim.

Just a bit further on, **Kamináki** is a strong contender in the sweepstakes for 'Corfu's most terrifying beach descent'. There are two tavernas, a small water-sports facility and around

100m (330ft) of attractive white-pebble beach. The next beach along the road is home to the large Nisáki Beach Hotel. You will have to share the pebbles with hotel guests but the beach is of reasonable size, and there are good water-sports facilities.

Drive a little further, and at a tight hairpin turn there are signs pointing down to **Agní**. Parking at the road's end is limited, so in peak season it's best to arrive at Agní by boat from Nisáki or Kalámi. Agní is a glorious spot, known to lots of happy diners, many of whom come here year after year to the three excellent tavernas that sit right on the picturesque beach.

Lawrence Durrell's beloved 'White House' still stands at the peaceful far side of **Kalámi**. It is now part holiday lodgings, part taverna, where you can enjoy the marvellous landscape that inspired him to write *Prospero's Cell* (a hugely

A Glimpse of Albania

All along its northeast coast, Corfu looks across at the mainland of Albania. At its nearest point – on the stretch between Kalámi and Ágios Stéfanos – the shore of this mysterious ex-communist land is less than 3km (2 miles) away.

With the return of relative calm to the country after the turbulent mid-1990s, day trips to Albania are again a popular outing. The boat journey from Kérkyra Town to the Albanian port of Sarandë (Agía Saránda; 35–75 minutes depending on craft used) costs about €34 for adults, with €19 extra charged for a highly recommended guided tour of ancient Butrint and buffet lunch. Agencies in every resort offer this excursion, but you'll only get the cheapest prices cited above by booking directly through the shipping company, Petrakis, at the New Port (tel: 26610 25317/38690; email: <petrakis_lines@aias.gr>). Sipa Tours (tel: 26610 56415, <www.sipatours.com>) has good one-, three-, and six-day tours taking in Butrint, the heritage town of Gjirokastro, and the Blue Eye beauty spot.

evocative holiday read that describes Corfu in the days before tourism) in 1939. Despite a number of vacation villas and an insensitive new hotel complex that defaces one side of the glorious steep and verdant hills enclosing the bay, it remains at heart a tranquil resort.

On the neighbouring bay, charming **Kouloúra** is scarcely large enough for a handful of fishing boats and a small taverna, but it is one of the most picturesque and photographed corners of Corfu. A constant stream of buses, cars and motorbikes pull up at the large parking space high above on the main road to gaze down on its classic, tiny horseshoe harbour enclosed by tall cypresses. There is not a more typically Ionian view in the archipelago. Gerald Durrell, the brother of Lawrence, lived in Kouloúra and, while there, penned the amusing *My Family and Other Animals*.

Just past Kouloúra, yet another lovely white-pebble beach, far below, beckons invitingly to drivers from the clifftop road. It belongs to **Kerasiá**, an attractive low-key resort with a handful of villas. It is reached by the turn-off to Ágios Stéfanos or, for the energetic, via a 20-minute coastal path from Kouloúra.

Ágios Stéfanos east is the most exclusive of this coast's beautiful bays. Fishing boats and yachts bob lazily in the circular harbour, ringed by whitewashed cottages and tavernas. Although each year this lovely resort becomes less of a secret, the relaxed atmosphere of a timeless fishing village prevails.

Not so long ago, **Kassiópi** was also a quiet fishing village. These days it's a highly popular little resort. In fact, Kassiópi

> **The northeast coast is sometimes dubbed 'Kensington-on-Sea' after the well-heeled British visitors who holiday here.**

was a thriving settlement even in Roman times, visited by Cicero, Cato and Emperor Nero, among others. It is named after the god Kassios Zeus, protector of the remote corners of the land,

Kassiópi, a fishing village with a long history, now a thriving resort

and the village church supposedly stands on the site of a temple built in his honour. Its successor, the delightful Church of Panagía Kassópitra (Our Lady of Kassiópi), used to be the foremost shrine on Corfu before the arrival of St Spyrídon. Its icons attest to the many miracles worked here. Opposite the church, the Angevins built a now-ruined medieval fortress during the 13th century to provide protection against barbarian raiders.

The town is increasingly packed with tourists during the summer peak, but the horseshoe-shaped harbour is still home to local fishermen. Nightlife is lively and Kassiópi has something of a party image with its tacky tourist bars. However, there are still several passably authentic Greek restaurants. Bathing beaches lie to either side of the resort, especially just west of the port, along the castle headland.

The spectacular coast road ends just before Kassiópi, and beyond it the scenery alters. Softer, shrub-covered foothills

Belfry at deserted Paleó Períthia

border a broad coastal plain blessed with an abundance of hayfields, vines and almond trees. Here the first sandy beach, **Kalamáki**, appears. Tour operators run excursions to 'Sandy Beach', as they have renamed it, but in reality it is an unattractive place, as dull as its grey sand. Give it a miss and continue to **Ágios Spyrídonos**, 3km (1¼ miles) further northwest. This pretty, small beach with fine golden sand is something of a secret, with just one taverna and a handful of villas.

An interesting break from the seaside is provided by the 'ghost town' of **Paleó Períthia** (Old Períthia), set on the northern slopes of Mt Pandokrátor and accessible by a turning opposite the road to Ágios Spyrídon. (Maps showing the road as unpaved are out of date.) Incredibly, Períthia was once the capital of Kassiópi Province. Today there are just a handful of families resident in summer, operating a few tavernas with a beautiful view of the crumbling village and, above it, Mt Pandokrátor. Simply sitting and savouring the peace and quiet here makes a journey well worthwhile.

No natural disaster overtook Paleó Períthia, its residents simply moved to the coast in search of work. Overgrown footpaths between the crumbling stone houses and churches provide a haunting glimpse of old Corfiot life. In spring this valley is a great spot for naturalists, who can spot hundreds of butterflies, birds and wild flowers. There is a path to the top of Mt Pandokrátor from here; the climb takes about an hour.

THE NORTH

The shores of the north coast boast an 8-km (5-mile) expanse of sand stretching from Cape Róda through Acharávi and beyond to Cape Agías Ekaterínis. Although the width of the beach and its sand quality varies, the sea is very shallow for a long way out, making it popular with young families.

From the main highway, a number of side roads go down to Almyrós beach, where a large resort development is underway. Further on, don't be put off by the roadside sprawl of tourist facilities at **Acharávi**. The side roads leading to its long beach are lush with olive and citrus trees, giving this relatively new resort much laid-back charm, as does the 'Old Village' on the south side of the road, opposite the water pump. There are good restaurants and tavernas.

Sidári's rock formations

The neighbouring resort of **Róda** is quite heavily developed with several older buildings, narrow streets, and a pretty little square still surviving among the tavernas, gift shops and touristy bars and restaurants. The remains of the 5th-century BC Doric temple of Apollo have been discovered here but, despite a signpost, there is nothing to see.

The booming resort of **Sidári**, 39km (24 miles) from Kérkyra Town, is by far the most developed on the north coast and its main street reflects many of the less savoury aspects of mass tourism on the island. Nonetheless, even in the middle of such a relentless onslaught, a picturesque little village square survives. Its charming church is worth a visit. The broad, sandy main beach has very shallow warm water and a wide range of water sports. Sidári's finest feature, however, is the series of striking **rock formations** that rise out of the sea at the western end of the resort.

The striated sandstone here is continuously carved by the wind and the sea into sandy coves with caves and ledges (some of which are very good for diving). There are a number of adjacent bays to explore, becoming more spectacular the further west you go. At the last bay you can go no further and, for your own safety, a fence blocks the top of the bluff. The view from here – of the giant cliffs tumbling straight down into the sea – is breathtaking.

From Sidári (and also from Ágios Stéfanos), boat trips run to the three small islands lying to the northwest, known collectively as the **Diapóndia Islands**. They are Mathráki, Eríkoussa and Othoní and are famous for their fishing grounds. **Othoní** is the largest, and the westernmost point of Greece, but is rarely visited as a day trip; **Eríkoussa** has the

Channel of Love

The most famous of Sidári's many rock formations is the Canal d'Amour. Legend has it that anyone who swims through this narrow channel (when the water is in shade, according to some versions) will find the man or woman of their dreams. The problem is that the original Canal d'Amour, topped by a sea arch, collapsed long ago, and today nobody can quite decide which is the 'official' Canal d'Amour. If you are in search of love, take no chances and swim through them all.

best sandy beach and attracts the most visitors; **Mathráki** is the smallest, has a sandy beach and is also an excursion destination. Each island has at least one taverna and one place to stay overnight.

Stunning views of the northwestern tip of Corfu await at **Perouládes**, 2km (1¼ miles) west of Sidári. Bear right at the end of the village, following the signs to the Sunset Taverna. At the end of the track, a flight of steps

Perouládes panorama

leading down to a narrow beach reveals a glorious view of sheer, gold-grey striated cliffs plunging to the water, bordered by a delightful fringe of dark sand. There are no facilities on the beach itself, but the Panorama Restaurant and Seventh Heaven Bar on the clifftop provides a fantastic place to watch the sunset. From the village, you can follow a track out to Cape Drástis, the island's northwestern tip, where you'll discover a pretty cove and more interesting offshore rock formations.

THE NORTHWEST

Ágios Stéfanos west (not to be confused with Ágios Stéfanos on the east coast), also called San Stefano, is a developing resort with a long, wide beach of compacted sand and pebbles ending at white cliffs. It is popular with windsurfers and is still relatively uncrowded. Adjacent to the resort is a classic horseshoe-shaped fishing harbour where trips depart to the Diapóndia Islands. A path leads out to the headland, which is the westernmost point of Corfu.

A 45-minute clifftop walk to the south leads to **Arílas**, in the next bay (you can also drive there). This low-key resort is smaller and slightly prettier than many developments and has an attractive sandy beach that shelves gently into the sea.

A classic crescent-shaped beach of coarse sand stretches about 3km (1¾ miles) around the bay at **Ágios Geórgios north** and gives this burgeoning resort a lovely setting. Water sports are available, though the water is deeper and consequently often colder than at most other places on the island. There are stunning views over the bay from the cliffs at Afiónas, a picturesque village above Ágios Geórgios.

Paleokastrítsa

You can reach the most celebrated beauty spot on the island by a fast, paved road from Kérkyra Town; the distance is 25km (16 miles). In the 1820s **Paleokastrítsa** was a favourite picnic spot for High Commissioner Sir Frederick Adam, and it is said that he had the first road built across Corfu especially to reach it. (To justify the expense he proposed constructing a military convalescent home there, but it was never built.)

Several small coves with incredibly clear turquoise water nestle in a coastline of hills and promontories draped in olive, cypress and lemon trees. Strips of partly sandy, partly shingle beach ring the shoreline, and sea grottoes yawning out of sheer cliffs provide employment for the local boatmen who ferry visitors to and fro. Further out to sea, a large ship-shaped rock known as Kolóvri is said to be the petrified Phaeacian ship that once bore Ulysses home.

Many claim that Paleokastrítsa was the site of the reputedly fabulous palace of King Alkinoös. Its magnificent setting is indeed fit for a king.

'Paleó', as it is often called, was never a village itself but merely the port of the hilltown of Lákones.

The year-round population is said to be less than 50, but this is hard to believe during the high season, when several hundred Corfiots move down from their hillside homes to cater for the crowds that flock to this scenic spot.

Fortunately, no building has been permitted to crowd the bright little **monastery** (open daily 7am–1pm and 3pm–8pm; free) that perches on the main, wooded promontory. You must dress appropriately to enter, and suitable wraps are provided at the gate for women. Established during the 13th century after the discovery

Paleokastrítsa's monastery

here of an icon of the Virgin Mary, the monastery was rebuilt following a fire in the 17th century. Today it is a lovely, peaceful haven, and many thousands of rolls of film have been expended on its delightful patio, where a charming, creamy-yellow, typically Ionian belltower decked with pink bougainvillea is set off by a brilliant blue sky. Its three bells represent the Holy Trinity. Visit in the evening when there are few visitors and the soft light is at its best.

A tiny museum harbours ancient icons, vestments and various oddities, including an old olive press, huge wine barrels, a giant clam and some enormous bones. 'Part of the skeleton of a huge sea monster which was killed by the crew of a French ship in 1860 in the waters by the monastery', enthuses

Pink rocks and deep-blue 'eyes'

the caption on the latter item. The poor creature was in fact probably a whale. As you enter the monastery church, you may be given a candle to light; a donation is expected. Do make sure you visit the monastery shop before leaving. It is a lovely place to browse or buy.

Paleó's main beach of Ágios Spyrídonas is the most crowded, but from here you can take boat excursions to Corfu's only sea caves and grottoes, with their mysterious pink rocks and blue 'eyes' – extremely deep holes that, with the play of sunlight, turn an incredibly deep blue colour. A longer trip can be made north from Paleokastrítsa to Ágios Geórgios – a beautiful voyage, chugging past jagged cliffs that dwarf your tiny vessel. If you are lucky, you might see the dolphins that often cavort in these waters.

The finest view of Paleokastrítsa is from a lookout point high above the coastline. A narrow asphalt road twists up through several hairpin bends to the precariously perched village of Lákones. A little further on, at a café called – with some understatement – Bella Vista, is a magnificent panorama that ranks among the finest in Europe.

From Paleokastrítsa ('Little Old Castle') you can see the massive walls of **Angelókastro** (open daily May–Sept 8.30am–3pm; entrance fee), the medieval fortress constructed by Michael Angelos Komnenos in the 13th century. In 1537 several thousand Corfiots held out against Ottoman attack in this impregnable citadel. From the car park at the foot of the castle, it is a steep, 20-minute climb to the summit. Little is left inside the walls beyond a small church and some cisterns, but the views from here are marvellous and – in a nice piece of historical symmetry – extend eastward to Kérkyra Town's Old Fort. In the lower keep, look for the cave-chapel of Agía Kyriakí, with hermit cells carved out of the rock and traces of frescoes.

Continue on to **Makrádes**, where the main road is lined with souvenir stalls and tavernas catering to tour buses. The village itself (off a side road to the left) is a brightly whitewashed cluster of houses with many picturesque corners. Just beyond Makrádes, follow the steep, but completely paved road to **Pági**. The first reward is the stunning vista of Ágios Geórgios Bay you get before you arrive. The second is the timeless mountain village itself, crowned by an Ionian belfry.

The huge Angelókastro fortress

Alternatively, you can continue along the main road as far as scenic **Troumbétas Pass**. *Troumbétas* means 'trumpet', and the pass is so called after the musically minded officer in charge of the road construction team who liked to stand on the pass above and blow his trumpet to call the crew to lunch. From here you can head north to Sidári or Róda, or return to Kérkyra Town via Skriperó.

THE WEST

The wide Rópa Valley separates Paleokastrítsa from the central and southern beaches of the west coast. This former marsh was drained by the Italians during their brief occupation in World War II, and is now the island's agricultural heartland. Further south down the west coast lie Corfu's best beaches, with wide stretches of deep, golden sand.

The Rópa river flows down through the valley and out to the sea at **Érmones**, making the latter site yet another contender for the *Odyssey* legend of Odysseus being found by Nausika and her retinue. The bay is picturesque, but its small beach of shingle and pebble is not particularly attractive and is surrounded by hotel and bungalow developments. The main hotel runs a funicular service down to the beach.

By contrast, **Myrtiótissa** was described by Lawrence Durrell, nearly 70 years ago, as 'perhaps the loveliest beach in the world'. Perhaps, perhaps not – but at least few can deny it is the loveliest in Corfu and surely among the very best in all the Greek islands. Moreover, it is almost unchanged since Durrell's day, with just a couple of stalls selling drinks and renting umbrellas. Sheer cliffs covered with trees and shrubs drop directly to the sand, creating a sense of wonderful isolation that has led Myrtiótissa to become unofficially recognised as the island's nudist beach. Don't worry if you don't want to shed all your inhibitions: there are many more people here who are costumed than those who let it all hang out. The sand is soft and golden, and at both ends of the long beach curl rocky promontories offering marvellous snorkelling in crystal-blue water.

The side turning for Myrtiótissa is signposted at Kelliá, a village on the Pélekas–Vátos road. It's initially paved, but then increasingly rough and steep; most cars must be left about halfway along the 1.8km (1 mile) distance and the remainder covered on foot. There's no real parking or turning space at the bottom, and even motorbikes or scooters are challenged by the final grade. The beach is anyway getting too congested in peak season – enter into the original spirit of the place by walking the final stretch.

Adjacent to Myrtiótissa as the seagull flies, but a little way round by road, is another of the island's acclaimed beaches, **Glyfáda**. Against a backdrop of crumbling cliffs with rock formations at either end, this large sandy beach is one of the finest on the island. Swimming is superb; the water is initially shallow, but deepens further out. Beware, however, as there can be a strong undertow at the northern end (as on many beaches along the west coast). Unlike at Myrtiótissa, development at Glyfáda is fairly heavy. You'll find a few large hotels, several tavernas and all water sports. The beach is frequented by day-trippers from Kérkyra Town and other resorts.

Glyfáda's long sandy beach, one of the finest on the west coast

A traditional home in the unspoiled hill town of Sinarádes

A steep hill leads up from Glyfádha to the village of **Pélekas**. Today it is busy and commercialised, full of travel agencies, restaurants, discos and rooms for rent. Nonetheless, it is still an attractive place and makes a good coffee stop – if you can find a parking place. Follow signposts to the famous **Kaiser's Throne**, just above Pélekas. Set atop a high ridge, this is a panoramic viewpoint where the German emperor, Kaiser Wilhelm, built a small telescope point to watch the spectacular sunsets. From here, at certain times of the year, the sun appears to slide diagonally down the hillside and into the sea. The views are excellent, from Paleokastrítsa in the west to Kérkyra Town in the east.

Until quite recently, **Pélekas Beach** – one of the finest on the island, officially called Kondogialós – was (like Myrtiótissa) difficult to reach. Now a steep, narrow but paved road from Pélekas drops all the way down to the sea in a couple of minutes. Like Myrtiótissa and Glyfáda, the beach here is an idyllic, wide stretch of soft, golden sand with a rocky portion providing good snorkelling in crystal waters. With only a couple of tavernas, it is still largely undeveloped, but the price of its new paved road can be seen at the south end of the beach in the shape of a huge, white hotel complex.

The charmingly unspoiled hill town of **Sinarádes** lies 5km (3 miles) south of Pélekas. Go past the central square and opposite the Venetian-style church tower you'll see signs to the **History and Folklore Museum of Central Corfu** (open Mon–Sat 9.30am–2pm; entrance fee). Set in a traditional Corfiot house, this is an authentic reconstruction of a village home *circa* 1860–1960 and features two floors of furniture, costumes, craftsman's tools and other artefacts. The star exhibit is a *papyrella,* a reed boat (like those of ancient Egypt) used on Corfu from prehistoric times until 1950. Take time to wander around the pretty flower-decked village and enjoy its quiet atmosphere.

The scenic bay of **Ágios Górdis**, surrounded by verdant slopes covered with orchards, olive groves and market gardens, is punctuated by a gigantic erect rock rising from the water at the southern end – an excellent spot for snorkelling, as are the rocks at the northern end. The long sand-and-shingle beach gets very crowded in high season.

EXCURSIONS

Both the idyllic island of Paxí (the ancient Paxos) and the nearby Greek mainland are easily accessible for day trips. Corfu travel agents can provide you with information on such excursions and on ferry schedules if you wish to stay longer.

Paxí

One of the most delightful island experiences in the Mediterranean awaits you just 10 nautical miles south of Corfu. **Paxí**, the smallest of the seven principal Ionian Islands, starts its seduction even before your boat docks, with dark green hills and astonishingly clear aquamarine waters.

This tiny, verdant island – approximately 11km (7 miles) long and 5km (3 miles) wide – has some 300,000 olive trees and 1,500 permanent residents. It is famous for the quality of its olive oil; to this day Paxí earns almost as much from olives as from tourism. This quiet, relatively uncommercialised island is wonderfully tidy – there is virtually no litter or roadside rubbish, while houses, villas, shops and restaurants are maintained and painted as if in preparation for a competition for the best-kept Greek island.

The clear, limpid waters off Paxí are irresistible. The island has no natural sandy beaches, though off the shingle strip at Lákka the bottom is pure sand. However, you'll find excellent swimming from flat rocks and numerous pebbly coves around the shoreline, even if many are secluded and accessible only by boat. There is a small strip of imported sand on the islet of Mogonísi in the far south, but it is nearly always crowded.

The sea caves in the towering cliffs along the west coast are truly spectacular, and the blue water there is so dazzling in its intensity that snorkelling is something you won't soon forget. The sea depth off these sheer rocks plunges from 25m to 90m (82ft to 295ft), with fish of varying sizes gliding along in schools, at different levels. The largest of these caves,

A Chip off the Old Block

According to Greek mythology, the sea god Poseidon created Paxí by striking off the southern part of Corfu to make a retreat for himself and his mistress, Amphitriti. Circe, the enchantress who in Homer's Odyssey detained Ulysses on her island and turned his men into swine, supposedly came from Paxí.

Ypapandí, was said to be Poseidon's home. A modern legend has it that a British submarine hid here for many months during World War II, venturing out on occasion to conduct its valiant operations. Soaring out of the sea along this stunning coast is the massive hulk of **Orthólithos** – a huge finger of rock that has been hewn out of the cliff face by the elements.

The clear-blue waters of Paxí

Peaceful Paxí often appeals to those who want to get away from it all. But this can be difficult in midsummer, especially in the first three weeks of August, when the tiny island becomes a magnet for Italian tourists. Then, prices swell accordingly and accommodation is heavily booked. The island has only two large hotel complexes; other accommodation is in fairly upmarket villas and apartments, though visitors who want to stay only a few nights can often find rooms to rent in private houses. However, in high season it's sensible to book accommodation in advance.

If you are a day-tripper you only get to spend a couple of hours here. Normally you have a choice of an island tour by minibus or a speedboat tour of the caves. But to do the island justice, you should visit on a scheduled ferry and plan to stay at least two nights – enough time to see all the island's highlights and savour its relaxed atmosphere.

From Kérkyra Town, there are ferries to Paxí during the tourist season, but the schedules change frequently so enquire at the ferry agencies. The journey takes anywhere from 90 minutes (direct) to three hours (via Igoumenítsa). AirSea Lines (tel: 26610 49800/99316; <www.airsealines.com>) operates a daily seaplane service in the summer between Corfu and Paxí. There are also one-day excursions to Paxí and adjacent Andípaxi, most of which also visit Párga on the mainland. In the high season there is a daily *kaïki* service between Gáïos and Párga, taking around 75 minutes. More reliable are the daily car ferries which ply from Igoumenítsa, the mainland port opposite southern Corfu.

All boats arrive at **Gáïos**, the small quayside capital of the island. The pretty waterfront square is lined with tavernas, shops and charming weathered houses, while handsome yachts fill the harbour.

Longós, the smallest and prettiest of Paxí's three main villages

Any tour of this tiny island will also take in the coastal villages of Lákka and Longós. Both are delightful. **Lákka** is a pretty port situated around a horseshoe-shaped bay on the northern island shore, ideal for water sports. It's the island's sailing capital and has several charming cafés and tavernas as well as an aquarium displaying all the local marine life. Two of the best beaches are also here. From Lákka there is a pleasant walk to a

Life is unhurried on Paxi

lighthouse on the cliffs and – a bit further – to the inland monastery of **Ypapandí**, the oldest on the island, where a delightful belltower provides scenic views.

Longós (also called Loggós) is a tiny, traditional fishing village huddled around a lovely harbour. Here, too, you'll find numerous places to eat and drink.

There is a regular bus service between the three main settlements, though it operates only during the day and early evening. Scooter and motorbike hire is available. There are a handful of taxis, but it can be difficult (if not impossible) to find one late at night.

Walking around the island is sheer delight. Timeless tracks and paths along stone terraces and through mature olive groves end in idyllic hamlets. Along the roadsides you'll see abandoned stone cottages and old olive presses, as well as lovingly tended grape arbours, cacti and bougainvillea in profusion. The surrounding hillsides are dotted with round stone towers of ruined windmills missing their sails.

> **Between Magaziá and Fondána stands the island's largest olive tree – it takes five men with outstretched arms to embrace the huge twisted trunk. This giant stands in an incredible grove of 500-year-old trees, all still producing fruit faithfully every two years.**

A popular walk leads from Magaziá, in the centre of the island, up to the tidy hilltop cemetery at the Ágii Apóstoli (Holy Apostles) Church, where there is a striking view of the chalk-coloured Erimítis cliffs.

Andípaxi

Andípaxi (Antipaxos) is an undeveloped island about 5km (3 miles) to the south of Paxí. By sailing boat the journey from Gáïos takes 30 to 40 minutes. Cloaked in vineyards and lapped by transparent turquoise water, Andípaxi is occupied by only a handful of permanent residents but attracts plenty of visitors who converge on the island's two beaches. Vríka has an arc of fine, white sand in a little cove, with tavernas at either end and a few beach umbrellas for hire. The nearby bay of Vatoúmi has brilliant-white stones along its coastal strip but a soft, sandy bottom underwater; there's one taverna on the hillside, plus a newer one behind the beach.

Swimming at both Vríka and Vatoúmi is superb, but don't expect to enjoy this idyllic setting in solitude. Excursion boats continually drop off bathers throughout the day, and numerous private boats also moor offshore. In high season, these sweet little beaches are often sadly overcrowded.

Párga

Párga village occupies an exquisite seascape on mainland Greece's northwest coast, just east of Paxí. Its magnificent crescent bay is backed by verdant hillsides and dotted by off-shore islands. As you enter by sea, watch for the tiny island of Panagía, just off Kryonéri beach, crowned by a lonely church.

Like Corfu, this is by no means 'untouched Greece'. Párga has been very commercialised for many years, with a profusion of restaurants, bars and tourist shops, none of which are terribly different from those in Corfu. Yet, even after the picturesque, quiet charms of Paxí (excursion boats often visit the two consecutively, so comparison is inevitable), Párga is still a delight. Its spectacular setting and views and quiet narrow whitewashed streets have an appeal all their own.

A Venetian castle built in 1624 looms above the promontory immediately to the north of the town. The climb up Párga's steep streets to the castle is actually shorter than it looks from below and well worth the effort for the stupendous views.

Be sure to follow the path around the crest of the hill for a look at the high-walled ruins and for additional views of the next bay, **Váltos**, which is home to a long, splendid golden-sand beach.

One of Párga's steep streets

If you have a day or two to spend in Párga, take the popular boat trip up River Ahérondas (Acheron), thought to be the mythological River Styx – the gateway to the Underworld. It concludes at the Necromantion, the Oracle of the Dead. Here, in an underground chamber, the ancient Greeks sought contact with the souls of the departed, under the auspices of the local priests of Hades, the Lord of the Underworld.

WHAT TO DO

SHOPPING

Prices are rising in Greece, and as a result you shouldn't expect great bargains on Corfu. In souvenir and gift shops you might find that some good-natured bargaining is tolerated if you are buying more than one item or spending a reasonable amount – but don't push it. Local profit margins have to cover not only the tourist months but also the off season, when shops are often closed. Corfu is not the Middle East or Asia, and some shops have even put up signs saying 'Fixed Prices' or 'No Bargaining'.

If you are not a resident of the EU, you might be able to claim back the 18 percent VAT (sales tax) included in the price of most goods (if you spend over a certain amount). Ask for details at shops with 'Tax-Free for Tourists' stickers.

Where to Shop

By far the best range and quality of shopping on the island are to be found in Kérkyra Town. Businesses open in the morning and, because of the ubiquitous 'siesta', close for a few hours in the afternoon. On Tuesday, Thursday and Friday all shops reopen at around 5pm and stay open until around 10pm. However, many shops are open only in the mornings on Monday, Wednesday and Saturday and don't reopen for the evening. In Kérkyra Town the elegant old-world atmosphere of evening shopping (even if you are only window-browsing) is not to be missed.

There are also a number of specialist workshop outlets on the road from Kérkyra Town to Paleokastrítsa or Róda. These are worth a visit, particularly the no-name olive-wood workshop just below Skriperó (look for the logs and power saws outside at the front).

Corfiot villages produce handmade lace and embroidery

Best Buys

Gifts from the olive tree. Corfu's most plentiful commodity – its olive trees – provides the basis for many fine souvenirs. Local artisans carve a variety of attractive bowls, platters, trays, utensils, statuettes, jewellery, toys and all sorts of other ingenious olive-wood oddities. However, there's more than wood to the venerable trees. The island's olives and high-quality olive oil are appreciated worldwide, and a small bar of olive-oil soap, often tastefully giftwrapped, is an ideal, inexpensive present.

Pottery, glass and ceramics. Corfu is home to many talented potters and craftspeople. You'll come across some lovely ceramics, including museum copies (the shop in the Old Fort specialises in the latter).

Gold and silver. Silversmiths still create bowls and trays using the old patterns of their Greek and Venetian ancestors, beating out the silver much as they would have done centuries ago. Many of the jewellery designs are based on traditional forms that reflect the development of Greek civilisation, including such classic symbols as the lion, dolphin, ram and bull. Voulgáreos Street, off the Liston, is the place to find silver in Kérkyra Town.

Leather. Leather is one of the few areas where you can still get real bargains on Corfu. Goods such as handbags, sandals, wallets and belts are often very good buys in Kérkyra Town. Agíon Pándon Street is home to many young and creative fashion designers.

Weaving and embroidery. There's a good selection of handwoven and embroidered items. Colourful woollen shoulder bags called *tagári*, handwoven floor mats in muted colours, tablecloths, napkins, aprons, skirts and blouses of lace and cotton (in particular those woven in Corfiot villages) are always popular. The best buys in this category are probably cotton needlework shawls and bedspreads. The village of Kassiópi is home to a traditional industry of lace and crocheted goods, with the late Princess Margaret among its former customers.

Reproduction icons. These are on sale all over Kérkyra Town and range greatly in price according to size and quality. Icons are also sold at the monasteries at Mt Pandokrátor and Paleokastrítsa (the latter is a particularly attractive place to shop).

Other specialities. Kumquat liqueur is a speciality made from a small Japanese citrus fruit grown on Corfu. There are medium and dry

Look for jewellery in ancient and modern designs

varieties of this sweet, orange-coloured drink, though the clear-coloured extract is considered the best quality. It is sold throughout Corfu, and the Mavromatis factory on the Paleokastrítsa road is a popular stop with tour groups. You can also sample kumquats in the form of crystallised fruits.

Another particularly sweet treat worth trying is nougat of almonds or sugared nuts. In addition, the richness of the island's flora ensures that its famous honey always possesses a distinctive character. In the fruit and vegetable markets look for bags of herbs and spices.

Corfu has its own wine producers and you can purchase a number of local vintages on the island. Other drinks available include *oúzo* (the national drink) and Greek brandy. The most famous brandy is Metaxa, which is rated from three to seven stars according to its quality and strength. Most local alcoholic drinks are very reasonably priced.

Other typically Greek souvenir ideas include strands of worry beads *(kombolóïa)*; tapes or CDs of Greek folk songs; elaborate skewers for *souvláki*; or a *bríkia*, a long-stemmed copper coffee pot used for making real Greek coffee, which also makes a nice ornament.

ENTERTAINMENT

Greek Music and Dance

The Corfiots' love of good music and dance runs deep. Wherever you are staying, you will almost certainly come across a 'Greek Night', which generally comprises a (more-or-less) traditional meal, Corfiot music (usually live) and dancing. It is of course the latter that everyone comes to see. Traditional Corfiot and national Greek dances are taught at an early age, and the dancers – be they specially hired performers, restaurant staff or simply locals who want to do their bit – can almost always be relied on for an energetic performance.

Song and dance in traditional dress is usual at village festivals

Whereas some Greek island dances are a little staid, the Corfiot interpretation can be particularly exciting. Corfiot males revel in athletic, virile, fast dances with high-kicking Cossack-like steps and not a little bravado. Dancing in a ring of fire to the accompaniment of plate-smashing is quite typical. Another dance involves picking up a glass of wine with the mouth (no hands allowed) from a press-up position. The wine is downed with a jerk of the neck; more macho types bite a chunk out of the empty glass before tossing it contemptuously aside.

Another crowd pleaser is the *zeïbékikos*. The spectators, clapping in time to the music, cheer on the dancer, who bends back and seems to pick up a heavy table only with his teeth. (He's actually taking the table's weight on his chest and stomach.) Not content with picking up a mere empty table, expert practitioners extend this feat to a table with a chair on top, and some go for broke by getting a young child to sit on the chair on top of the table. It has to be seen to be believed. By the end of the night, it is a fair bet that the dancers will have cajoled everyone up on to the floor to join in a version of the *syrtáki*, Greece's best-known group dance; steps are simplified for visitors.

These dances are usually all accompanied by the famous eight-stringed mandolin, the *bouzoúki*, which for many foreigners has become synonymous with all Greek music. In fact, the instrument (which is of Middle Eastern origin) is a comparatively recent import to the island, though the haunting melodies of Manos Hadjidakis and Mikis Theodorakis have made it an intrinsic part of Greek – and Corfiot – folklore.

Greek Easter

Kérkyra Town is famous for staging the most colourful Easter (Páskha) celebration in Greece. Here it is often called Labrí ('brilliance'), and the spectacle attracts throngs of Athenians and other mainlanders. Every church has its Good Friday procession. The best starts after nightfall, departing from the cathedral with the bishop, dignitaries and Corfu's famous town bands.

On Holy Saturday morning, the body of the patron saint, Spyrídon, is paraded at length around town. The spectacular pomp honours his miraculous intervention in 1553, which saved Corfu from famine. Then, at 11am, police clear the streets. Suddenly pottery, old plates, vases and other breakables are hurled from the upper stories of houses. One theory behind this old and unique Corfu custom is that it is supposed to show anger at Judas' betrayal of Jesus.

At midnight, when the bishop intones *'Hristós anésti'* ('Christ is risen'), every electric light goes on, fireworks soar overhead, church bells ring and – most memorably – everyone lights a candle. Easter has arrived. On Easter Sunday wine flows like water and men perform traditional Greek and Corfiot dances.

Authentic performances of songs and dances are staged at village festivals throughout the season, where young and old alike participate, dressed in the traditional costumes of their ancestors. If there is not one in your locality during your holiday, make the trip into Kérkyra Town on Tuesday evenings in summer. 'Cultural Evenings' are held in the Town Hall Square, Agíou Spyrídonos Square and Spiliá Square, featuring folk dancing, classical music

A dancer in Corfiot costume

and traditional music with a choir (all start at 8pm). Music, dance and folklore performances are also staged regularly in the New Fort. The dancers are a lovely sight in all their finery, even if you don't experience the rough-and-ready excitement of taverna dancing.

Corfu is indeed a very musical island. Part of the Venetian legacy means that Kérkyra Town alone boasts three orchestras, with at least a dozen more spread over the island, representing in all more than 750 musicians, as well as a municipal choir and a chamber-music group; it is claimed that nearly half the Athens Symphony Orchestra is Corfu Conservatory-trained. Marching bands are a regular fixture at festivals, and Sunday concerts often take place during the summer on the Esplanade. The New Fort also hosts guitar recitals, jazz performances and classical concerts. Theatre lovers should note that there are regular summer performances (often of ancient Greek plays), either in one of Kérkyra Town's two fortresses or at the Mon Repos outdoor theatre.

For details of all concerts, traditional festivals and theatre pick up the cultural-events leaflet from the airport or the local tourist information office.

Other Nightlife

All the major resorts around the island have music bars, karaoke bars, clubs and discos. Kávos is home to the island's youngest and wildest nightlife, followed by Ýpsos/Pyrgí and Sidári. Kérkyra Town has a lively nightlife strip of its own, placed discretely just outside the centre along the main road just west of the New Port, which is worth the short taxi ride if you're staying anywhere between Gouviá and Pyrgí.

The island has one casino (tel: 26610 46941), housed at the Corfu Holiday Palace (formerly the Hilton) in Kanóni. It is open from 8pm until 2am and offers roulette, blackjack, baccarat and chemin de fer. You must be 18 to enter and everyone has to show a passport. Men are required to wear a jacket and tie.

SPORTS AND RECREATION

Snorkelling and diving. Water of excellent quality laps the island's innumerable rocky inlets, and you will find small, fascinating sea grottoes and offshore rocks by Paleokastrítsa, Sidári and Perouládes. Paleokastrítsa, in fact, is considered to be one of Europe's best locations. Don't be put off by eelgrass at certain east-coast points; some of the most colourful fish lurk where eelgrass thrives. Corfu's coastal waters are deep and clear, allowing divers some superb views. All scuba-diving schools have qualified instructors who will choose dive locations according to the amount of experience

> The best way to enjoy the coastline is by boat. You can rent all types of motorboats, from a small outboard to a 10-m (33-ft) caique.

you have. Extended boat trips are available for advanced divers. For the more advanced trips, or to hire equipment and go by yourself, you will need to show a diving certificate. Most major resorts have reputable diving schools.

Water sports. Corfu has numerous schools where you can learn to water-ski. Avoid the northern shore, however, as the winds here can be too strong. Boards and sails for windsurfing are available for hire at nearly every beach on the island where the right conditions prevail, and instruction is offered at many places.

Explore the coast by caique

Parasailing, now very popular, is available at several beaches, as is jet-skiing. The major water-sports centres are at Dassiá and Ýpsos, though water-skiing and windsurfing are available almost everywhere.

Golf. The highly acclaimed Corfu Golf Club (tel: 26630 94220) is rated as one of the best courses in the Mediterranean. It is situated next to Érmones, in the Rópa Valley. The 18-hole course is likened to a links course, with water hazards and a design that provide a real challenge for seasoned golfers. You can arrange lessons with qualified pros (it's best to book ahead); clubs and other essentials are available for hire. You'll also find a good shop and clubhouse with a bar and restaurant.

Non-golfers can enjoy a bit of horseback riding at the Rópa Valley Riding Stables (same phone number as the golf course), offering one- to two-hour rides in this beautiful valley.

Cricket. Cricket was introduced by the English and is now an integral part of Corfu's summer scene. Matches take place regularly in the new cricket ground at Gouvia Marina on Saturday and Sunday afternoons, usually attracting enthusiastic spectators. Corfu clubs frequently play against visiting teams from Britain and Malta, among others. The season's top tournament is the European Cricket Championship (ECC), which involves teams from seven countries and is contested in mid-September. There is another pitch at the Rópa Golf Club, while youth teams play at the pitch on the Esplanade in Kérkyra Town. If you are a keen cricketer, it may be possible to play with one of the Corfu teams (tel: 26610 47753).

ACTIVITIES FOR CHILDREN

Corfu is a very popular holiday spot for families, and most resorts and newer hotels are designed with children in mind. Many larger hotels have separate, shallow children's swimming pools and play areas, and most of the more luxurious hotels have special games and activity programmes.

While most beaches are perfectly safe for children, those with sandy shores and very shallow water will be most appealing to families with very young children. These include Róda, Sidári, Acharávi, Aríllas and Kávos, though the latter is also known for its gregarious nightlife.

Kérkyra Town is largely for adults, but kids might enjoy a ride around town in the colourful 19th-century horsedrawn carriages. The *Kalypsó Star* glass-bottomed boat leaves the Old Port regularly for a 50-minute trip around Vídos Island, where (caged) sea lions perform for the passengers. In Paleokastrítsa the short boat trip to the caves and grottoes is also a winner with kids.

Giant slides and 'hydrotubes' at Aqualand water park

The most popular children's day out (and a great day for all splashaholics) is at the Aqualand water park, with many thrill rides, the gentle 'Lazy River', the bouncy castle, swimming pools and special children's play area. Located at Ágios Ioán-nis, in the centre of the island some 12km (7½ miles) west of Kérkyra Town, the park is open daily from April to October. It's quite expensive, but children under four are admitted free and there are reduced rates after 3pm. Special buses make the trip from all over the island. More recently, a rival water-park – Hydropolis – has opened at Acharávi.

If your children love nature and horses, take them pony-trekking, a good outing for the whole family. This can be booked through most tourist agencies.

Most children love the spectacle of 'Greek Night' enter-tainment, with whirling dancers, rings of fire, smashing plates, tables picked up with teeth and other denture-defying acts. Most Greek Nights start at around 10pm.

it is not so much where you eat as what you eat (fish, for example, is usually expensive) that will decide the amount of the bill. A service charge is included, but diners normally leave between five and ten percent extra for the waiter.

Corfiots, like most other Greeks, enjoy their food warm rather than piping hot. Casserole dishes such as *mousakás* might be cooked at lunchtime and either kept warm all day or just reheated at night. If you like your food hot or if you are concerned about the hygiene implications of re-heating, you should order grilled dishes in the evening.

WHAT TO EAT

Fast Food

For snacks or even lunch, many holidaymakers follow local example and pop into a bakery for a freshly baked *fílo*-pastry pie filled with cheese, a *tyrópita*; the *fílo*-less version looking like a turnover, called *kourá*, is less messy and more cheese-filled; if it's filled with spinach, it's a *spanakópita*.

Another cheap takeaway option is a *gýros*, better known to Western Europeans as a *doner kebab*. Pressed meat is sliced off a vertically rotating spit and stuffed into *píta* bread with some salad, a yoghurt dressing and a handful of chips. Then there is *souvláki:* a kebab of grilled cubes of meat, grilled over charcoal and served in the same fashion. *Souvláki* is also popular served as a main course in restaurants and tavernas.

Appetisers

There are a great many ways to start your meal. For a little of everything, try a plate of mixed appetizers *(pikilía mezédes)*.

Dolmádes are vine leaves that have been stuffed with rice and then seasoned with grated onion and herbs; sometimes this is meat-free – ask. *Melitzánes tiganités* are slices of aubergine (eggplant) fried in batter; *kolokythákia tiganitá* are

Eating outside is the norm during summer months

courgette (zucchini) fritters. Another popular starter is *saganáki* (fried cheese), though confusingly the term can also mean a cheese-based red sauce used over mussels and shrimp.

The Greeks have a great predilection for dips. The commonest are the following: *tzatzíki*, yoghurt with crushed garlic and grated or finely sliced cucumbers; *taramosaláta*, a smooth, pink paste made from grey mullet roe, mashed potatoes or moistened bread, olive oil and lemon juice; and *melitzanosaláta*, a purple-brown mush of grilled aubergine, onions, olive oil and garlic. Dips are served with local bread, which varies in quality – darker village bread is excellent.

Horiátiki saláta ('village salad') is the proper term for the ubiquitous 'Greek salad', eaten either as a starter or with the main course. It comprises tomatoes, sliced peeled cucumber, mild onions, black olives and green peppers, topped with a thick slice or two of white feta cheese, drizzled with olive oil and dusted with oregano.

Fish and Seafood

Fresh fish abounds, but the seas around Corfu have been almost exhausted and restaurant prices are likely to shock
many visitors. These are often quoted by weight, so to avoid
any unpleasant shocks at the end of your meal establish what
the price is before ordering. You should watch the fish being
weighed (uncleaned) and confirm the weight to avoid fiddles.

A seafood speciality here is the pleasantly piquant *bourd-
éto*: white-fleshed fish in a sauce of tomato, red pepper and
olive oil. *Bianco* (sometimes called *bouillabaisse*) is a catch-
all name for a stew of local fish, potatoes, white wine,
lemon, garlic, black pepper, onions and whatever else the
chef fancies throwing in.

There are several varieties of the bream family, such as
the tasty *melanoúri* (saddled bream) or *sargós* (white
bream). *Barboúni* (red mullet), a Mediterranean favourite,

Corfu's local wines, served by the carafe, are often surprisingly good

is a popular fish on Corfu. Most fish are served simply grilled. More familiar are *fangrí* (red porgy), *glóssa* (sole), *sinagrída* (dentex) and *xifías* (swordfish). A typical (though not exclusively Corfiot) accompaniment to battered fish is *skordaliá*, a garlic and breadcrumb purée.

Seafood starters include *kalamarákia* (squid) fried in batter; *maridákia* (picarel) is also generally deep fried. *Garídes* (prawns, shrimp) are often served *saganáki* style, in a piquant cheese-laced red sauce; *htapódi krasáto* means octopus stewed in wine until the whole mix is a dark pink colour.

If you tire of local fare, you can usually find (not too far away) everything from gourmet cuisine to ethnic fare, from hamburgers to crêpes. Don't turn your nose up at Italian food in particular – the Greeks love pizza and pasta, and the large number of Italian visitors demand high standards in summer.

Meat Dishes

Mousakás is perhaps the most popular of all Greek dishes (pronounced 'moo-sah-**kas**' rather than 'moo-**sah**-kas'). It is a layered dish of minced meat (traditionally lamb), aubergine (eggplant), potatoes, a bechamel-type sauce and spices.

The Greeks love lamb. *Kléftiko* is traditional Greek oven-roasted lamb, though in Corfu the dish might be served in a sauce of wine, vegetables and yoghurt. Another popular lamb dish is *arní frikassé*, stewed with green vegetables. Less common is *gástra*: lamb baked in white-wine sauce with garlic and red peppers.

Sofríto is an island special comprising slices of beef or veal stewed in a sauce of white wine, garlic and wine vinegar with a touch of black pepper. *Stifádo* is beef stewed with baby onions in a finely spiced tomato sauce – something of an island speciality, though it is available all over Greece.

Stámna is another beef casserole, baked with courgettes (zucchini), peppers and cheese in a ceramic dish.

More adventurous diners might like to try *kokorétsi*: spiced sausages of innards flavoured with herbs. *Keftédes* are Greek meatballs, usually made from minced beef or lamb, breadcrumbs and egg, then flavoured with grated onion, spices and herbs. One of the cheapest menu items is *kotópoulo* (chicken), often simply roasted on a spit over charcoal. Pork usually comes simply as *brizóles* (pork chops), but lamb chops are called *païdakia*.

Pasta Dishes
The Greeks and especially the Corfiots are very fond of pasta. *Pastítsio* is made with layers of minced meat, tomato, macaroni and bechamel sauce topped with cheese. *Gouvétsi* is a combination of meat (usually lamb) and *kritharáki* pasta (identical to Italian *orzo*), baked in a clay casserole. Don't confuse *pastítsio* with *pastitsáda;* the latter is beef stewed in a richly flavoured tomato sauce, served with pasta.

Vegetables
Vegetarians are not restricted to yoghurt and Greek salad. You'll usually find *hórta* (spinach-like wild greens); *fasólia* (butter beans), often described as *gígandes* ('giant beans') and served in a tomato-and-onion sauce; and *fasolákia* (string beans). Not to be missed is *briám*, often described as 'Greek ratatouille', made of aubergine, potatoes, courgettes, tomatoes, onions and olive oil; it's served as an appetiser, side dish or main course (perhaps topped with cheese and breadcrumbs).

Desserts
Sweets are just that – and usually sticky as well. The most famous is *baklavás*, a flaky, paper-thin *fílo* pastry filled with chopped almonds and walnuts and drenched in honey or syrup.

Similar is *kataïfi*, a pastry that resembles shredded wheat. You will not see these in a restaurant or taverna. Look instead in bakeries or in a *zaharoplastío*, a café/patisserie (rarely found outside Kérkyra Town). Yet another mouthwatering speciality is *loukoumádes*, a sweet, puffy deep fried dough ball dipped in syrup. It is often sold by street vendors.

A much healthier food is Corfu honey (*méli*), which makes a wonderful breakfast snack poured on to the island's local yoghurt (*giaoúrti*). You'll find this on restaurant menus, usually with nuts added for a bit of

Local produce for sale

crunch and extra flavour. It's delicious with fruit.

Corfu's magnificent wild strawberries (*fráoules*), which appear in May and June, are another of the tastiest treats in the Ionian. However, for much of the summer the only fruits that appear on the restaurant table are yellow melons, watermelons and grapes.

WHAT TO DRINK

Coffee

If you order simply 'coffee', you might be offered the traditional Greek brew, *kafés ellinikós* – a thick, strong concoction brewed to order in a long-handled copper or aluminium

Making coffee the Greek way

pot called a *bríki* and poured (grounds and all) into a tiny cup. 'Greek' coffee – really generic Middle Eastern coffee renamed in a fit of patriotic pique after the various Cyprus crises – is served very sweet *(glykós)*, medium *(métrios*, the most common option) or unsweetened *(skétos)*, always accompanied by a glass of chilled water.

Instant coffee is generically known as *nes* or *néskafe*, irrespective of the brand; it's pretty vile, an extra-strength formula for Mediterranean tastes that can provoke migraines in the susceptible. In recent years there has been a backlash against it, and in large resorts and Kérkyra Town you can easily find proper brewed coffee *(gallikós* or *fíltro)*, as well as competently executed cappuccino and espresso. *Fredduccino* – cold cappuccino – is also increasingly popular. Any milky coffee is *me gála*.

A real treat in hot weather, and quite a fashionable drink too, is *frappé* – Greek iced instant coffee. The milky version looks a little like a small Guinness and tastes like a coffee milkshake, but it's surprisingly refreshing. Most Corfiots drink their *frappé* black.

Alcoholic Drinks

Oúzo, the national aniseed-flavoured apéritif made from distilled grape detritus, is very often taken neat *(skéto)* on Corfu. When you add the cold water that always accompanies it, the *oúzo* turns milky – and becomes less potent.

Corfu produces a reasonable quantity of local wine, but much of this is kept by the vineyard owners for their own private use. Usually light red *(kokkinéli)* or deep purple in colour, it is best drunk cool from the cellar, where it sits in wooden casks.

House wine is often surprisingly tasty and worth trying before paying more for bottled wine from the mainland. Among local bottled wines, the rarest and most expensive is Theotóki, a dry white produced solely from grapes cultivated in the Rópa Valley. More common is the wide range of mainland Greek wines to choose from. Three top-class reds are Averof Katógi, Tsantali Rapsáni and almost anything from Nemea. Those who prefer a premium white might try Gentilini Robola from neighbouring Kefalloniá, Spyropoulos from the Peloponnese, Athanasiadi (central Greece) and Lazaridhi (Macedonia). At the end of a meal, Mavrodáfni – a sweet red similar to Marsala – is a good choice.

Retsína is an acquired taste and it's less popular on Corfu than elsewhere in Greece. But you'll have no trouble finding this inexpensive pine-resin flavoured white wine.

The Ionian Islands are well known for their liqueurs. The speciality of Corfu is *koum kouat* (kumquat), a syrupy concoction that is produced from miniature kumquats, citrus fruits grown here far from their native Japan.

The common drinking toasts are '*Yámas*!' or '*Yássas*!' ('To your health!').

Ginger Beer

Kérkyra Town is the only place in Greece where you can get genuine 19th-century-style ginger beer, a delightful relic of British colonial rule. Locally called *tsitsibýra* (pronounced 'tsin-tsi-BEE-ra'), it should be served well chilled and is extremely refreshing in hot weather.

To Help You Order...

Could we have a table?	Boroúme na éhoume éna trapézi?
I'd like a/an/some…	Tha íthela…

beer	**mía býra**	bread	**psomí**
water	**neró**	coffee	**éna kafé**
(iced)	**(pagoméno)**	dessert	**éna glykó**
cutlery	**maheropírouna**	fish	**psári**
milk	**gála**	fruit	**froúta**
salad	**mía saláta**	glass	**éna potíri**
salt	**aláti**	ice cream	**éna pagotó**
soup	**mía soúpa**	meat	**kréas**
sugar	**záhari**	napkin	**hartopetséta**
tea	**éna tsáï**	potatoes	**patátes**
wine	**krasí**	rice	**rýzi**

...and Read the Menu

barboúnia	red mullet
briám	'Greek ratatouille'
dolmádes	stuffed vine leaves
fasólia	beans
garídes	prawns
htapódi	octopus
keftédes	meatballs
kléftiko	roast lamb
kotópoulo	chicken
marídes	whitebait
pastítsio	macaroni pie
sofríto	veal stew
souvláki	kebab
stifádo	stew (usually beef) with tomatoes

HANDY TRAVEL TIPS

An A–Z Summary of Practical Information

A

ACCOMMODATION

Many hotels are heavily booked with package tours from mid-June until mid-September, especially during the first three weeks of August. Reservations are strongly recommended. If you do arrive without one, try the travel agencies in the resorts or Kérkyra Town. They may know of available accommodation. The tourist police also keep a list of accommodation and may be able to point you in the right direction.

Prices are controlled according to a rating system based on a building's age, facilities, amenities and other factors. Hotels are rated from A to E (rooms in categories A and B have private bathrooms), but prices can vary widely within each category. Luxury establishments, rated L, are not price-controlled. A star system, designed to replace the letter scheme, was introduced in 2003 but has met resistance; 5-star is equivalent to L, 4-star is A-class, and so on.

In high summer some form of air conditioning is vital for a good night's sleep. If your room doesn't have air conditioning (and many older properties don't), you can rent fans locally.

Villas and Apartments. Corfu has more villas, apartments and studios (the latter terms are interchangeable) to rent than many other Greek tourist centres. Accommodation ranges from simple rooms to lavishly appointed summer homes – often tastefully converted from a traditional house or houses – complete with swimming pool. In the UK, four companies specialise in top-of-the-range secluded luxury villas on both Corfu and Paxí: CV Travel (tel: 0870 606 0013), Sunvil (tel: 020 8568 4499), Simpson Travel (tel: 0845 811 6502) and Travel à la Carte (tel: 01635 863 030). More affordable are Meon Villas (with a good selection of villas across the island; tel: 0870 909 7550), Direct Greece (with nice properties on the northeast coast at very reasonable prices and excellent representatives on the ground; tel: 0870 191 9244),

Thomson Villas with Pools (tel: 0870 167 6548) and Simply Travel (tel: 0870 166 4979).

Rooms in Private Homes. The cheapest rooms are those that are privately rented. They are almost always clean, and are graded A and B by the local tourist police, though rates are often negotiable.

I'd like a single/double room **Tha íthela éna monóklino/díklino**
  with bath/shower   **me bánio/dous**
What's the rate per night?   **Póso éki/stihízi gia káthe vrádi?**

AIRPORT

Located only 1km (0.6 mile) from the capital, Corfu's lagoon-side airport is capable of handling all but the largest jets. However, time spent here can sometimes be frustrating, with long waits for baggage and other inconveniences.

Here are some tips for surviving the airport departure pandemonium. Take your own drinks and sandwiches, as delays are commonplace and the refreshment outlets may not be able to cope with backlogs of passengers awaiting their flights. Facilities and seating in the airside lounge are inadequate, so the best place to find a space to sit down – often on the floor – is at the far end of the Arrivals hall.

The terminal building has shops, car-hire desks and refreshment stands. The currency-exchange office opens at 9am and remains in operation until 2am if there are international flights scheduled to land late at night. (It's a good idea to buy a few euros before you travel, in case the airport office is closed, though there is at least one ATM in the airport.)

There is no bus service linking the airport with Kérkyra Town. Taxis in theory are cheap, but be warned that overcharging on the airport route is common. Agree a price in advance.

For general airport information, tel: 26610 30180. Olympic Airways, tel: 26610 38694. Aegean Airlines, tel: 26610 27100.

B

BICYCLE AND MOTORCYCLE HIRE

You can hire bicycles and motorcycles in all the tourist centres. However, many package operators warn clients against motorised cycles and scooters for the quite legitimate fear of an accident (and to drum up more business for organised excursions). It is vital that you check that motorbike hire does not invalidate your holiday insurance. Scooter hire is cheap (you should be quoted a rate per day, including third-party insurance and CDW, collision-damage waiver).

Terms vary by operator. Usually, to hire a motorbike with an engine larger than 50 cc you must be at least 18 years old and hold a full motorcycle licence. It is illegal to ride without a crash helmet, or to drive without an appropriate licence on your person – the spot fines issued at the many checkpoints approach €100.

It is certainly not advisable to ride a motorbike in shorts or a swimsuit, since burns or scrapes resulting from even a slight accident could be appalling. Inspect brakes and tyres before hiring, and drive with care. Even on good roads there are occasional potholes.

Bicycle hire is less common, largely because of Corfu's mountainous terrain, but a good place for serious bikers is the Corfu Mountain Bike Shop (tel: 26610 93344 or 26610 97609), on the main road at Dassiá. It offers top-quality bikes and can also organise expeditions.

| What's the hire charge for a full day? | **Póso kostízi giá mía méra?** |

BUDGETING FOR YOUR TRIP

Corfu is certainly not the cheapest of the Greek islands. It is probably as costly as most other Mediterranean destinations. In high season, the rate for a good four-star hotel is around €130 minimum per night for a double room. Booking an airfare/accommodation package will make a substantial saving.

Dining is not as cheap as you might think, with a three-course meal plus drinks in a decent restaurant or taverna costing around €17–28 per person. Car hire starts from about €30 per day in low season (including fully comprehensive insurance). Public transport and museum fees are inexpensive.

C

CAMPING

Camping in Greece is permitted at official sites only. There are 10 sites on Corfu, all north of Kérkyra Town, open at least from April to October. For the list, contact the tourist police or travel agencies.

May we camp here?	**Boroúme na kataskinósoume edó?**
We have a tent	**Éhoume mía skiní**

CAR HIRE

It is definitely worth hiring a car in order to explore the wonderful island scenery. As elsewhere in Greece, this is not particularly cheap, but it is certainly less expensive than touring by taxi. And public transport is inadequate for island sightseeing. For a decent family-sized car in high season, you should budget around €300 per week. In high summer choose a model with air conditioning.

You'll find car-hire firms at the airport and throughout the island, especially in tourist centres. To be on the safe side, reserve a car ahead of time – especially for the high season. Local firms generally charge slightly less than international agencies and provide equally good cars and service. International chains present on Corfu, bookable through their websites, include Avis, Hertz, Europcar, National, Sixt and Budget.

You will need a credit card for the deposit and a full national licence (held for at least one year) from your country of residence. Depending on the model and the hire company, the minimum age for hiring a car varies from 21 to 25. Third-party liability insurance (CDW) is usually included in the stated rate, and it is always worth paying a little more for comprehensive coverage.

I'd like to hire a car (tomorrow)	**Tha íthela na nikiáso éna avtokínito (ávrio)**

CLIMATE

July and August are the sunniest, hottest and busiest tourist months. You may prefer to stay between mid-May and late June or from early September to mid-October. At any time outside July (even in August) it might rain. Corfu is, after all, one of the greenest of all the Greek islands.

In winter it rains very hard. November and December are the wettest months and January the coldest, but even during these mid-winter doldrums the climate is temperate. Spring, when Corfu bursts with wild flowers, is the best time for walking.

The chart shows each month's average air and sea temperature in Celsius and Fahrenheit, and the average number of hours of sunshine per day.

	J	F	M	A	M	J	J	A	S	O	N	D
Air °C	10	10	12	15	19	24	27	26	23	19	15	12
Air °F	50	50	54	59	66	75	81	79	73	66	59	54
Sea °C	15	15	15	16	18	21	24	25	24	21	19	18
Sea °F	59	59	59	61	64	70	75	77	75	70	66	64
Sunshine hours	5	6	7	7	9	10	11	12	9	6	4	3

CLOTHING

Clothing is almost always casual on Corfu. Unless you plan to frequent the casino, you can leave ties and fancy dresses at home. However, it is quite nice to dress up a little for a night in Kérkyra Town. With regard to warmth, choose lightweight cotton clothing in spring and summer, and a warm jacket, sweater and rainwear in autumn and winter. Since it rains from time to time on Corfu, a protective coat or umbrella is a good idea – except for July. Plastic sandals are useful for stony beaches.

CRIME AND SAFETY (see also EMERGENCIES and POLICE)

The Corfiots, like the vast majority of Greek people, are scrupulously honest. However, unfortunately thefts occur more often than they used to on the island, so it's sensible to leave valuables in the hotel safe. Take care of your passport – but at the same time be aware that you're required to have official ID on your person at all times in Greece.

Possession of drugs is a serious matter in Greece. Make sure you have a prescription from your doctor if you will be carrying syringes, insulin, any narcotic drugs or even codeine, which is illegal in Greece.

Any fears about the proximity of Corfu to Albania and unrest in the Balkans are, for most holidaymakers, groundless.

CUSTOMS AND ENTRY REQUIREMENTS

EU citizens can enter Greece for an unlimited length of time. British citizens must have a valid passport. Citizens of Ireland can enter with a valid identity card or passport.

Citizens of the US, Canada, Australia and New Zealand can stay for up to three months on production of a valid passport. South African citizens can stay for up to two months on production of a valid passport. No visas are needed for these stays. If you wish to extend these timescales you must obtain a permit from the proper department of the Kérkyra Town police station.

Greece has strict regulations about importing drugs. All the obvious ones are illegal, and there are strong punitive measures for anyone breaking the rules. Codeine and some tranquillisers are also banned. If you take any drug on the advice of your doctor, carry enough for your needs in an official container – medicines for personal use are permitted.

Since the abolition of duty-free allowances for all EU countries, all goods brought into Greece from Britain and Ireland must be duty-paid. In theory there are no limitations to the amount of duty-paid goods that can be brought into the country. However, cigarettes and most spirits are much cheaper in Greece than in Britain and Ireland (government duty is much lower, so waiting until you reach your destination to buy these goods will save you money).

For citizens of non-EU countries, allowances for duty-free goods brought into Greece are: 200 cigarettes or 50 cigars or 250g of tobacco; 1 litre of spirits or 4 litres of wine; 250ml of cologne or 50ml of perfume.

Non-EU residents can claim back Value Added Tax (currently between 6 and 18 percent) on any items costing over €120, provided they export the item within 90 days of purchase. Tax-free forms are available at tourist shops and department stores. Keep the receipt and form. Make your claim at the customs area of the airport when departing.

Currency Restrictions. There are no limits on the amount of euros visitors can import or export. There are no restrictions on travellers' cheques, but cash sums of more than $10,000 or its equivalent should be declared on entry.

D

DRIVING

Road Conditions. Main roads are generally very good, though curves in the road are often indicated too late, sometimes unsignposted and never banked. If there is a mirror on a bend, slow down to low gear – it is probably going to be extremely tight or narrow, or perhaps both.

On many clifftop roads it is very dangerous to pass, so be patient if there is a slow-moving bus or heavy vehicle in front of you. Conversely, try to let local speed maniacs pass you as soon as it is safe to do so.

Secondary roads are some of the narrowest in any of the Greek islands – it's difficult to safely exceed 50kph – while anything marked 'unsurfaced' on a map can be very rough indeed. Rock-slides are common in the rainy season, and broken shoulders or potholes are not unknown on even the best-paved stretches. Drive with extreme caution, as you might be responsible for damage sustained to the underside of your hire car, even with comprehensive coverage.

Driving Regulations. Drive on the right side and pass on the left. Traffic from the right has right of way. If a driver flashes the lights, it means 'Stay where you are, I'm coming through', not 'Go ahead'. Seat belts are obligatory as is the carrying of your driving licence while at the wheel – an €86 spot fine at the many checkpoints if you are caught without it. The speed limit is 80kph (50mph) inside built-up areas, 100kph (62mph) outside. In practice, however, Corfu's winding roads usually set the speed limit.

Fuel. Unless you are on the top of Mt Pandokrátor, you will never be far from a filling station. However, in rural areas they are open only until about 7pm and closed on Sunday. On busy main roads and in resorts they open daily from early until late.

If You Need Help. For breakdown and accident assistance phone the Greek motoring club (ELPA) at 26610 39504. In case of road emergency, dial 104. Some car-hire companies have agreements with other roadside emergency companies, such as Hellas Service (tel: 157).

Road Signs. On main roads and at junctions these are in Greek and Latin (Western) letters; on secondary roads they may just be in Greek.

Detour	Παράκαψη/**Parákapsi**
Parking	Πάρκιγκ/**Párking**
No parking	...απαγορέυεται/**...apagorévetai**
Be careful	Προσοχή/**Prosohí**
Bus stop	Στάση λεοφορίο/**Stasí leoforío**
Stop	Σταμάτα/**Stamáta**
Pedestrians	Για πεζούς/**Gia pezoús**
Danger	Κίνδινος, επικίνδινος/**Kíndinos, epikíndinos**
No entry	Απαγορέυεται η είσοδος/**Apagorévetai i eísodos**

Are we on the right road for...?	**Eímaste sto sostó drómo gia...?**
Fill the tank please, with (unleaded) petrol	**Parakaló, geméste i dexamení me amólivdi**
My car has broken down	**To avtokínito mou éhi ragisméni**
There's been an accident	**Eínai distíhimai**

E

ELECTRICITY

Corfu has 220-volt/50-cycle AC current. Sockets are two-pin, so bring an adapter or transformer with you as necessary.

a transformer	**énas metashimatistís**
an adapter	**énas prosarmostís**

EMBASSIES AND CONSULATES *(presvía; proxenío)*

There are United Kingdom and Republic of Ireland consular offices in Kérkyra Town. Embassies of all major countries are located in Athens. From outside Greece, dial the country code 30 before the 10-digit number.

British Consulate: corner of Alexándras Avenue and Menekrátous Street (on seafront), Kérkyra Town; tel: 26610 30055.

Irish Consulate: 20a Kapodistríou Street, Kérkyra Town; tel: 26610 33411.

Embassies:

Australia: D. Soútsou 37, 115 21 Athens; tel: 21064 50404.

Canada: Gennadíou 4, 115 21 Athens; tel: 21072 73400.

Ireland: Vassiléos Konstantínou 7, 106 74 Athens; tel: 21072 32771.

New Zealand: 76 Kifissias Avenue, 11526 Ambelokipi, Athens; tel: 21069 24136.

South Africa: Leofóros Kifissías 60, 151 25 Maroússi, Athens; tel: 21061 06645.

UK: Ploutárchou 1, 106 75 Athens; tel: 21072 72600.

US: Vassilísis Sofías 91, 115 21 Athens; tel: 21072 12951.

EMERGENCIES

Police (Kérkyra Town), all-purpose emergency number, tel: **100**.
Tourist Police, tel: 26610 30265.
Kérkyra Town Hospital, tel: 26610 45811/5 (5 lines).
Ambulance, tel: **166**. Fire, tel: **199**.
Vehicle emergency, tel: **104** or **157**.

Fire!	**Fotiá!**
Help!	**Voíthia!**
Police!	**Astynomía!**
Stop!	**Stamatíste!**

G

GETTING THERE

It is possible to cross Europe overland and take the ferry from Italy to Corfu. But for most visitors, air travel is the only practical route. Most take charter flights from the UK, which link a dozen British airports to Corfu (around 3 hours' flight time). The only regularly scheduled flights to Corfu on commercial carriers depart from Athens (45 minutes). If you are travelling from North America, you might find it just as cheap to fly to London and pick up a charter flight from there.

GUIDES AND TOURS *(xenagí; periodíes)*

Authorised multilingual guide-interpreters work through hotels and travel agencies. Contact the EOT office or the Association of Corfu Travel Agents *(see Tourist Information on page 125)*.

Among the numerous tours offered are those to Paleokastrítsa, the Achilleion and Kérkyra Town, as well as 'Greek Nights', boat trips and day trips to Paxí and mainland Greece. You can book these and other tours through travel agents.

We'd like an English-speaking guide	**Tha thélame éna xenagó pou milái angliká**

H

HEALTH AND MEDICAL CARE

EU citizens with a European Health Insurance Card (EHIC), obtainable in their own country, can get free treatment under the Greek health service. However, you are likely to receive the minimum treatment and must pay for medication, and state hospital facilities are over-stretched in the tourist season. It's essential to obtain private medical insurance for your holiday. Doctors and dentists are concentrated in

Kérkyra Town; your hotel or apartment owner will be able to find you one who speaks English. Most resorts have a local medical clinic.

Hospitals. The capital's hospital and clinics operate a 24-hour emergency service (tel: 166) that dispatches ambulances to any point on the island with admirable speed. Otherwise, call the tourist police (tel: 26610 30265). Corfu General Hospital is situated on Polykroníou Konstandá Street in Kérkyra Town (tel: 26610 45811/7). Corfu Private General Clinic is located on the main Paleokastrítsa Road, just outside Kérkyra Town centre (tel: 26610 36044 or 26610 22946).

Pharmacies (ΦΑΡΜΑΚΕΙΟ – *farmakío* in singular). A red or green cross on a white background identifies a chemist (pharmacy). They are normally open only during the morning Monday to Friday, but a notice on the door should tell you the nearest one for after-hours service. One pharmacy is always open in Kérkyra Town at night and on Saturday and Sunday. Without a prescription, you can't get sleeping pills, barbiturates, or medicine for stomach upsets.

Mosquitoes (non-malarial) can be a nuisance on Corfu, so bring along mosquito repellent. Or you can buy small electric devices that you plug in at night to keep the bugs at bay.

a doctor/dentist	**énas giatrós/odontogiatrós**
hospital	**nosokomío**
an upset stomach	**varystomahiá**
sunstroke	**ilíasi**
a fever	**pyretós**

HOLIDAYS

Banks, offices and shops are closed on the following national holidays, as well as during some feasts and festivals *(see also page 92)*:

1 January	*Protokroniá*	New Year's Day
6 January	*Ágia Theofánia*	Epiphany

25 March	*Ikostipémpti Martíou (tou Evangelismoú)*	Greek Independence Day
1 May	*Protomagiá*	May Day
15 August	*Dekapendávgoustos (tis Panagías)*	Assumption Day
28 October	*Ikostiogdóïs Oktovríou*	Óhi ('No') Day, celebrating defiance of the 1940 Italian ultimatum
25 December	*Khristoúgenna*	Christmas Day
26 December	*Sýnaxi Theotókou*	Meeting of Virgin's Entourage

Moveable dates:

Katharí Deftéra	1st day of Lent: 'Clean Monday'
Megáli Paraskeví	Good Friday
Pásha	Easter
tou Agíou Pnévmatos	Whit (Pentecost) Sunday and Monday ('Holy Spirit'), June

Note: These moveable holidays are celebrated according to dates in the Greek Orthodox calendar, which often differ from Catholic or Protestant dates.

L

LANGUAGE

Only in remote countryside spots will non-Greek-speaking tourists run into serious communication problems. You will find that basic English is spoken almost everywhere, as are Italian, German and French, to some degree.

Stress is a very important feature of the Greek language, denoted by an accent above the vowel of the syllable to be emphasised.

The table on page 117 lists the Greek letters in their upper- and lower-case forms, followed by the closest individual or combined letters to which they correspond in the English language.

A	α	a	as in *father*
B	β	v	as in *veto*
Γ	γ	g or gh	as in *go* (except before *i* and *e* sounds, when it's like the *y* in *yes*)
Δ	δ	d	sounds like **th** in *this*
E	ε	e	as in *get*
Z	ζ	z	as in English
H	η	i	as in *ski*
Θ	θ	th	as in *thin*
I	ι	i	as in *ski*
K	κ	k	as in English
Λ	λ	l	as in English
M	μ	m	as in English
N	ν	n	as in English
Ξ	ξ	x	as in *box*
O	ο	o	as in *top*
Π	π	p	as in English
P	ρ	r	as in English
Σ	σ	s	as in *kiss*, except like *z* before m or g sounds
T	τ	t	as in English
Y	υ	y	as in *country*
Φ	φ	f	as in English
X	χ	h	as in Scottish *loch*
Ψ	ψ	ps	as in *tipsy*
Ω	ω	o	as in *long*

M

MEDIA

Bookshop. The best English-language stock on the island is at Melpo Tourmousoglou, at Nikifórou Theotóki 47, with maps, guides and coffee-table publications on Corfu, as well as novels for beach-reading.

Internet Cafés. Internet access is now available in almost every beach resort. In Kérkyra Town try www.netoikos at Kalohairetou 12–14, behind the Alpha Bank on Kapodistriou. Charges are typically €2 to €4 per hour.

Newspapers and Magazines *(evimerídes; periodiká)*. During the tourist season, foreign-language newspapers are on sale at shops and kiosks on the island, generally on the day after publication. The only Greek English-language paper is *The Athens News* (€1.50, every Friday); locally produced *The Corfiot* (€2, monthly) is heavily slanted towards property sales and advertorial restaurant reviews. The free monthly *Liston* is much better value, with interesting features.

Television *(tiliérasi)*. Most hotels and many bars offer satellite television networks, including CNN, BBC World and Sky.

Radio. BBC World Service is broadcast on the short-wave band (try 15.07 MHz and 12.09 MHz), but reception is poor.

MONEY

Currency *(nómisma)*. In common with most other Western European countries, the euro (EUR or €) is the official currency used in Greece. Notes are denominated as 5, 10, 20, 50, 100 and 500 euros; coins as 1 and 2 euros and 1, 2, 5, 10, 20 and 50 cents.

Banks and Currency Exchange: You'll find banks in Kérkyra Town and in the larger resort areas. Hotels and travel agencies (the latter sometimes called 'tourist offices') are authorised to change money, but you will probably get less for your money than you would from a bank. You'll need your passport as identification to change travellers cheques (but not to change cash).

ATMs. The easiest method to obtain cash is through 'hole-in-the-wall' cash dispensers. These can be found in Kérkyra Town and in all of the larger resorts. Depending upon your own individual card fees, this might also be the cheapest way to get money.

Credit Cards *(pistotikés kártes).* The major credit cards are accepted in many shops and by car-hire firms, most hotels, more expensive restaurants and some (but not all) filling stations. Be aware that you might have to pay an additional 5 to 7 percent for the privilege of using plastic. They are also not very cost-effective for use in ATMs, attracting fees of about 4 to 5 percent.

Travellers Cheques. Most major brands of travellers cheques – in any Western currency – are readily cashed. Always take your passport for identification.

I want to change some pounds/dollars travellers cheques	**Thélo na alláxo merikés líres/meriká dollária taxidiotikés epitagés**
Can I pay with this credit card?	**Boró na pliróso me aftí tin pistotikí kárta?**

O

OPENING HOURS

The siesta (the traditional Mediterranean lunchtime break) is still alive and well in Corfu, observed more strictly outside tourist areas.

Shops. Traditional hours are generally Mon–Sat 8.30 or 9am–2 or 2.30pm. On Tues, Thurs and Fri shops reopen in the evening from 5.30 or 6pm until 8.30–9pm. Shops catering to tourists often stay open through the siesta and until late each evening in the summer, as well as part of Sunday. Larger supermarkets open Mon–Fri 8.30am–8.30pm and Sat 9am–6pm.

Museums and Tourist Attractions. Hours vary greatly, but it is worth noting that Kérkyra Town's three main state-run museums are closed on Monday. Museums are typically open Tues–Sat 8.30am–3pm and Sun 8.30 or 9.30am–2.30 or 3pm.

Banks. Mon–Fri 8am–1 or 2pm.

Post Offices. Mon–Fri 7.30am–2pm (the main post office in Kérkyra Town closes at 8pm and is open Sat am in July and August).

Businesses and Offices. 8am–1pm, then 2pm–5pm. Government offices work 8am–1.30pm, sometimes 2.30pm, and don't reopen.

Restaurants and Tavernas. More traditional establishments open for lunch from noon until around 3.30pm and for dinner from 7pm to around 11pm. More tourist-oriented establishments might open early for breakfast or coffee and stay open throughout the day.

P

POLICE

Emergency telephone number, tel: **100**
Tourist police, tel: 26610 30265.

The tourist police *(touristikí astynomía)* have a specific mission to help visitors to the island, as well as to accompany state inspectors of hotels and restaurants to ensure that proper standards and prices are maintained.

If you need to report a loss or theft to the police, go to the police station closest to the scene of the crime. Each group of villages has a police station – you'll have to ask its location and go there.

Traffic police check car documents and driving licences, operate speed traps and issue fines for illegal parking (fines in Greece are high). Car-hire companies will use your credit-card details to pay ignored parking tickets; you have 10 working days to pay moving violations in person. Failing that, a court date will be set, and a summons sent to your home address. Failure to appear will result in an extra conviction for contempt of court, and make re-entry to Greece extremely awkward.

Where's the nearest police station?	**Pou íne to kondinótero astynomikó tmíma?**

POST OFFICES

Post offices handle letters, parcels and money orders, but no longer foreign currency exchange. Look for a blue sign with a Hermes head traced in yellow.

Post offices are generally open Mon–Fri 7.30am–2pm. The main post office on Corfu is in Kérkyra Town, at the corner of Alexándhras and Zafiropoúlou (tel: 26610 25544). It is open Mon–Fri 7.30am–8pm (until 2.30pm for money orders and parcels) and Saturday mornings during the months of July and August. Registered letters and parcels to non-EU destinations are checked before being sent, so don't seal them until presenting them at the desk.

Stamps are also sold at the majority of shops and hotels selling postcards. The price for sending a postcard to all overseas countries is €0.60. Delivery to Europe takes from 4 to 10 days.

Letter boxes are yellow, but make sure you use the one marked *exoterikó* (abroad). In tourist hotels, the receptionist will take care of dispatching your mail.

Have you received any mail for…?	**éhete grámmata giá…?**
A stamp for this letter/ postcard	**Éna grammatósimo giavtó to grámma/giavtí tin kart postál**
express (special delivery)	**katepígon**
registered	**systiméno**

PUBLIC TRANSPORT

Buses *(leofóría)*. The island's public bus service is not always efficient, but it is good value. Timetables are displayed at bus stops (ΣΤΑΣΙΣ – *stásis*) in the capital. They are also printed in *The Corfiot*. There are no all-night bus services. There are two types of buses on the island. The blue urban buses serve towns and villages in the vicinity of Kérkyra Town, including Benítses, Kondókali, Gouviá, Dassiá, the Achilleion and Pélekas. Buses for Kanóni depart from near the Esplanade. All other blue buses leave from San Rocco Square (tel: 26610 31595). Country buses are green-and-cream-coloured; they leave from the coach station on Avramíou Street, by the New Fort (tel: 26610 30627 or 26610 39985; <www.ktel.org>.

For all buses, buy your tickets on board or from kiosks in the square. You can flag a bus down anywhere within reason.

What's the fare to…?	**Póso éhi éna isitírio giá…?**
When's the next bus to…?	**Póte févgi to epómeno leoforío giá…?**

Taxis. Taxis based in Kérkyra Town are dark blue; those based in the country are grey. Taxi ranks in town are at the New Port, Old Port, Esplanade and San Rocco Square. There are two rates on the meter: a slow one used in Kérkyra Town and on two-way journeys, and a fast rate for single out-of-town trips or between midnight and 6am (the meter is changed from 'slow' to 'fast' at the town boundary). Check the fare before you get in the cab; if the meter is mysteriously 'broken', you will have to agree on a fare with the driver. Radio taxis can be summoned (tel: 26610 33811/2), for which there's a small surcharge; an advance appointment for a set time has a bigger surcharge, about €1.50.

Ferries. Regular ferries run to the Ionian Islands of Paxí and (in midsummer only) Kefalloniá. But the Ionians are not a group for island-hopping: it takes up to 3 hours just to sail to Paxí and 7 hours to Kefalloniá. To get to any other islands requires changing on the mainland, at Pátra. Ferries also go to various ports in Italy. All depart from Kérkyra Town, though there is an additional service to Igoumenítsa from Lefkímmi (near Kávos).

For current ferry schedules and fares check with your nearest travel agent or the port authority tel: 26610 32655.

R

RELIGION

The national religion of Greece is the Greek Orthodox Church. You must dress modestly to visit both churches and monasteries, which normally means long trousers for men, a long skirt for women and covered shoulders for both sexes. Men might be allowed to wear long shorts, and skirts might be provided for women to wrap around themselves.

Corfu's Catholics worship at the Church of Tenedos on Solomou Street in Kérkyra Town.

T

TELEPHONES

Local Calling. There are no longer any area codes as such in Greece – even within the same local-call zone you must dial all 10 digits of the number. What were the old codes are now merely the locators: 26610 for Kérkyra Town and the centre of the island, 26630 for northern Corfu, 26620 for the far south and 26510 for Paxí. For the local directory enquiries dial 131; for local operator assistance dial 151.

From Overseas. To call Corfu from abroad, first dial the international access code (00 from the UK), then **30** (the country code for Greece) and finally all 10 digits of the local number.

Long Distance from Corfu. International direct dialling is available at street-corner phones. These take phonecards, which are the cheapest (if noisiest) way to phone home. To reverse charges (collect calls), dial 151 for Europe and 161 for the rest of the world.

In higher-grade hotels you can dial long-distance from your room, but charges can be exorbitant – much more than using a mobile. Most visitors will find that using their home-based mobile is the best compromise between standing at a card phone or paying out for hotel surcharges. All UK providers have roaming agreements with at least one of the four Greek companies, contact your provider before travelling for more details. NOAH American users must have a tri-band mobile to get a signal in Greece. Overseas directory assistance is through the international operator (dial 161).

Fax Service. Fax services are available at major hotels, post offices and some travel agencies.

reverse-charge (collect) call	**plirotéo apó to paralípti**

TIME DIFFERENCES

Greek time is GMT +2. Daylight saving, when Greek clocks are put forward one hour, is observed from the last Sunday of March to the last Sunday of October. The chart shows the times in Corfu and various other cities in the European summer.

New York	London	**Corfu**	Jo'burg	Sydney	Auckland
5am	10am	**noon**	11am	8pm	9pm

TIPPING

The Greeks aren't tip-crazy, and the more remote the location the less likely it is that a tip is expected. Service may be included in the bill but it is the norm to leave a little more if service has been good.

Hotel porter	up to €2
Hotel maid	€1 per day
Waiter	5–10 percent
Taxi driver	10 percent
Hairdresser/barber	10 percent
Lavatory attendant	€0.30

TOILETS

Public conveniences are best avoided. But if you are desperate in Kérkyra Town, there are toilets at the following locations: Platía I. Theotóki, near the Esplanade bandstand, on Platía San Rocco and at Platía Spiliás near the Old Port. Take along your own toilet paper. It is considered polite to leave a small tip if there's someone in attendance.

A better option is to use facilities at museums or the better cafés. If you do drop in specifically to use the toilet, it's customary to purchase coffee or some other drink before leaving.

Note: you are always expected to put toilet tissue in the waste bin rather than down the toilet. Due to their narrow-bore pipes, toilets easily become clogged.

Where are the toilets?	**Pou íne i toualéttes?**

TOURIST INFORMATION

The Greek National Tourist Organization *(Ellinikós Organismós Tourismoú,* abbreviated EOT) has the following offices abroad:
Australia: 51–7 Pitt Street, Sydney, NSW 2000; tel: (02) 9241 1663.
Canada: 91 Scollard Street, 2nd Floor, Toronto, Ontario M5R 1GR; tel: (416) 968 2220.
UK: 4 Conduit Street, London W1R 0DJ; tel: 020-7734 5997.
US: 645 Fifth Avenue, New York, NY 10022; tel: (212) 421 5777.

These offices supply general information and glossy pictures, but when it comes to anything specific on Corfu they are usually of little help.

The island's tourist information office in Kérkyra Town has now closed and there are plans to open information kiosks around the town.

In the meantime, it is much easier to get local information from a travel agency (some of these actually call themselves 'tourist offices'). But you should remember that their information might not be impartial, as they have a vested interest in selling you excursions or at least in pointing you in certain directions. However, one agency that can be thoroughly recommended to vacationers in the northeast of the island is Travel Corner, in Kassiópi (tel: 26630 81220).

Where's the tourist office?	**Pou íne to grafío tourismoú?**

W

WATER

Tap water is not drinkable in much of the island: it comes from well bores which have been tainted by the sea (*glyfó* is Greek for brackish, a word you'll hear a lot). Always ask before using a tap. The few springs high in the hills are usually okay to collect from, but Kérkyra Town-dwellers are obliged to buy drinking water with a key-card from a pure fountain off Guildford Street.

WEBSITES

Many local Corfu travel agencies and hotels have their own websites, but these vary greatly in quality. A typical one is <www.corfuxenos.gr>; other useful sites include:
- <www.agni.gr>
- <www.corfuweb.gr>
- <www.terrakerkyra.gr>
- <www.travel-to-corfu.com>

Use a search engine and enter the words *Corfu travel* to locate these and other sites.

WEIGHTS AND MEASURES

Like most of Europe, Corfu uses the metric system.

Recommended Hotels

Most hotels in Corfu get booked up quickly for the high season: from mid-June until October and, in particular, around the middle of August. Make sure that you reserve well ahead *(see accommodation, page 104)*. To phone a hotel, dial the international country code for Greece (30), followed by the 10-digit number provided in our listings.

All hotels are classified by the Greek National Tourist Organization: luxury (L) class is at the very top, then A class down to E class (only hotels of L, A, B and C classes are featured below). In 2003, a star system (five-star equal to L, four-star to A, etc) was introduced, but has been slow to catch on. Rating establishes minimum price rates, but prices can often vary widely within each class according to the season, location and availability of rooms. By law, rates must always be posted in all rooms; in practice this is often ignored.

The price categories below are for a double room with bath (but without breakfast) in high season. All hotel room rates include VAT (Value Added Tax) of 18 percent. All listed hotels accept credit cards. All L- and A-class hotels have air conditioning; unless otherwise noted, it should be assumed that any other listed hotel does not have air conditioning. Many hotels in beach resorts are open only from April to October. Those in Kérkyra Town are open all year round.

€€€€	above 130 euros
€€€	90–130 euros
€€	60–90 euros
€	below 60 euros

KERKYRA TOWN

Arkadion €€€ *Kapodistríou 44, Kérkyra Town; tel: 26610 37670/2; fax: 26610 45087; <www.arcadionhotel.com>. B class/ 3-star.* A centrally situated six-storey hotel overlooking the arcades of the Listón and the Esplanade and four minutes' walk from the public beach. Air-conditioned rooms contain handmade Corfiot furniture and fine fabrics. Roof garden with splendid views, TV room, breakfast lounge and bar. 55 rooms.

Bella Venezia €€€ *N. Zambéli 4, Kérkyra Town; tel: 26610 46500 or 44290; fax: 26610 20708; <www.bellaveneziahotel.com>. B class/ 3-star.* Kérkyra Town's worst-kept secret, this comfortable hotel occupies a lovely, renovated neo-Classical Venetian building right in the centre of town. It's very popular with both Greek and foreign visitors. Excellent lobby and bar area plus an attractive garden terrace. Good staff and great value for the location. 32 rooms.

Cavalieri €€€ *Kapodistríou St. 4, Kérkyra Town; tel: 26610 39041; fax: 26610 39283; <www.cavalieri-hotel.com>. A class/ 4-star.* This converted six-storey 17th-century French nobleman's mansion, set at the end of the Esplanade, is a charming and comfortable place to stay in the centre of town. Worth a visit even if you are not staying here just to enjoy its roof garden's great views while nursing a not-too-overpriced drink. 50 air-conditioned rooms.

Corfu Palace Hotel €€€€ *Leofóros Dimokratías 2, Kérkyra Town; tel: 26610 39485; fax: 26610 31749; <www.corfupalace. com>. L class/5-star.* All rooms have a sea view in this graceful luxury hotel overlooking Garítsa Bay, just a 10-minute walk south of the Esplanade. Its beautiful grounds, featuring expansive lawns and subtropical gardens, border the old Venetian city walls. The hotel's many amenities include indoor and outdoor swimming pools, two restaurants and two bars. 115 rooms.

Konstantinoupolis €€ *Zavitsiánou 11, Old Port; tel: 26610 48716; fax: 26610 48718; <www.konstantinoupolis.com.gr>. C class/2-star.* A building dating from 1862, once a backpackers' dosshouse, now lovingly restored as a well-priced C-class hotel with sea and mountain views. Comfortable rooms and common areas, lift; open all year and thus heated. 31 rooms.

Palace Mon Repos €€€ *Anemómylos district, Garítsa Bay; tel: 26610 32783; fax: 26610 23459; <www.hotels-corfu.org>.*

B class/3-star. Renovated in the late 1990s, this hotel is the closest thing in Kérkyra Town to a beach resort. The swimming lido opposite is indifferent, but you have views to the sea, Old Fort, and Mon Repos woods, as well as a small swimming pool. À la carte restaurant and bar. Open May–October. 102 rooms.

THE SOUTH

Apollo Palace €€ *Mesongí; tel: 26610 75433; fax: 26610 75602. A class/4-star.* This attractive, modern, well-run hotel complex is set 100m (110yds) from the beach. It has its own gardens, pool, tennis court, restaurant, snack bar and two bars. Evening entertainment with live Greek music and dancing. Rooms are air-conditioned. 235 rooms. Open April–October.

Boúkari Beach € *Boúkari, 4km (2.5 miles) beyond Mesongí; tel: 26620 51791; fax: 26620 51792; <www.boukaribeach.gr>. A class apartments.* Two sets of sea-view units sleeping up to four for the price, with all amenities including coffee machines and air conditioning, a few paces from the excellent co-managed restaurant *(see page 138)*. Open April–October.

Corfu Holiday Palace €€€€ *Natsikás Street, Kanóni; tel: 26610 36540; fax: 26610 36551. L class/5-star.* Formerly the Hilton, this long-established deluxe hotel is set on a peninsula in lovely grounds, featuring the famous view of Mouse Island. Inside it is a large, older-style property with traditional furnishings, some stylish, some a little aged. It has its own secluded sandy beach plus two pools, tennis, ten-pin bowling, health-club facilities, restaurants, bars and the island's only casino. 305 rooms, including suites and bungalows.

Delfinia €€€ *Moraïtika; tel: 26610 76320; fax: 26610 75450; <www.delfiniahotels.gr>. A class/4-star.* Set next to a private beach in a shady olive grove with lemon trees and gardens of subtropical plants. All rooms have balconies. Facilities include a swimming pool, tennis courts, beach bars, fitness club and water sports. 83 rooms. Open April–October.

Golden Sands €€ *Ágios Geórgios south; tel: 26610 51225; fax: 26610 51140; <www.corfugoldensands.com>. B class/3-star.* Attractive low-rise hotel with a stylish interior set close to the main sandy beach, across the road from a small rocky cliff and four minutes' walk from the resort centre. The grounds feature small, well-kept lawns, two pools and a small children's playground. 83 rooms. Open April–October.

San Stéfano €€€ *Benítses; tel: 26610 71112; fax: 26610 71124; A class/4-star.* This modern, white hotel enjoys a wonderful site high on the hillside, next to the Achilleion Palace and above Benítses. Set in 14 hectares (35 acres) of private gardens, it was specially revamped as one of the host hotels for the 1994 EU summit, so rooms are excellent and include air conditioning. Facilities include the largest swimming pool on Corfu and tennis courts. 220 rooms, 30 bungalows. Open April–October.

NORTH OF KERKYRA TOWN

Casa Lucia €–€€ depending on cottage. *Sgómbou hamlet, At Km 12 of Kérkyra–Paleokastrítsa road; tel: 26610 91419; fax: 26610 91732; <www.casa-lucia-corfu.com>. A class rented rooms.* A restored olive-mill complex set among lovingly tended gardens with 10 units ranging from studios to family cottages. Most have kitchens, all share a large pool, though furnishings are resolutely 1980s. Peaceful setting at the very centre of the island makes this an excellent touring base. Open April–November.

Chandris Hotels €€€€ *Dassiá Bay; tel: 26610 97100; fax: 26610 93458; <www.chandris.gr>. A class/4-star.* Chandris operates two large, well-maintained hotels – the Corfu Chandris and the Dassiá Chandris – side by side on Dassiá Bay, separated from the sea by large private gardens. Rooms are in the main buildings, bungalows or chalets. Ask for a sea view to avoid a road-facing room. Facilities include air conditioning, swimming pool, tennis courts, restaurants and children's club. Corfu Chandris 301 rooms; Dassiá Chandris 251 rooms. Both hotels have wheelchair access. Open April–October.

Corfu Imperial €€€€ *Komméno; tel: 26610 91481; fax: 26610 91881; <www.grecotel.gr>. L class/5-star.* Set on its own secluded private peninsula with man-made sandy cove beaches, this luxurious hotel successfully mixes contemporary and classic elements and was one of the hosts of the 1994 EU summit. Considered one of the two or three top hotels on the island, it's a self-contained resort, with a huge seawater swimming pool, a wide range of water sports, a choice of restaurants and bars, a tennis club, health club and shops. Rooms are nicely furnished and are either in the main block or in bungalows dotted around the pretty grounds. 306 rooms. Open April–October.

Kontokali Bay Hotel €€€€ *Kondókali; tel: 26610 99000; fax: 26610 91901; <www.kontokalibay.com>. L class/5-star.* This modern, low-rise bungalow-style hotel boasts beautiful gardens next to a private sandy beach. Deluxe rooms are very well equipped. Facilities include a swimming pool, restaurant, beach bar, health club, tennis courts, water sports and an imaginative children's club. 152 rooms, 81 bungalows. Open April–October.

Louis Corcyra Beach Hotel €€€ *Gouviá; tel: 26610 90196; fax: 26610 91591; <www.louishotels.com>. A class/4-star.* This pleasant hotel-bungalow complex is right in the heart of the Gouviá resort but tucked away among well-tended lawns and gardens that slope down to a narrow, compacted-sand beach. Bedrooms and public areas, renovated in 1998, are stylish and well kept. Air conditioning is available in all rooms. Facilities include a pool, tennis courts, squash court, children's club and playground. 265 rooms. Open April–October.

Molfetta Beach Hotel €€ *Gouviá; tel: 26610 91915; <www. molfettabeach.com>. B class/3-star.* This small, friendly hotel is set in its own gardens along the main coast road. Each of the 27 rooms has a balcony with sea views. Open April–October.

Nefeli €€ *Komméno; tel: 26610 91033; fax: 26610 90290; <www.hotelnefeli.com>. B class/3-star.* An inland alternative to the Grecotel outfits, this small hotel in mock neo-Classical style, spread over three buildings among picturesque olive groves, has a loyal clientele and air conditioning in most units. Open April–October. 45 rooms.

THE NORTHEAST

Falcon Travel € apartments, €€ villas, €€€€ per week houses (2–4 persons; effectively e58–86 per night). *Nisáki; tel: 26630 81806; <www.falconcorfu.com>*. British-owned travel agency that controls a dozen beach-side apartments and villas in the area, and two sensitively restored houses which they own in the idyllic (and remote) Mt Pandokrátor hamlet of Tritsí. Car hire arranged for the latter; open April–October.

The White House €€ *Kalámi; tel/fax: 26630 91040; available through Direct Greece Holidays in the UK (see page 104); <www. white-house-corfu.gr>*. The ground floor of the famous White House, where Lawrence Durrell wrote *Prospero's Cell*, is now a taverna. The upstairs has been converted into a self-catering holiday home sleeping 4 to 8 people. Accommodation is comfortable, spacious and airy, with the original dining table and desk that Durrell used. The location (at the very end of the road in Kalámi) and views – across the bay and beach and out to Albania – are splendid. 4 rooms.

THE NORTH AND NORTHWEST

Roda Beach Village €€€€ *Róda; tel: 26630 64181; fax: 26630 63436; email: <midas@ath.forthnet.gr>*. *A class/4-star*. This was Róda's first hotel, last renovated in 1997. It is rather secluded from the town, with extensive gardens that lead down to the beach. It includes three swimming pools (one for children), tennis, a basic fitness room, restaurants and bar. 388 rooms, including 20 bungalows. Wheelchair access (partial).

Villa de Loulia €€€€ *Perouládes, 500m (545 yards) from beach; tel/fax: 26630 95394; fax: 26630 95145; email: <villadeloulia@ yahoo.com>*. *Special category*. One of Corfu's few rural restoration inns, this mansion dating from 1803 has been refurbished to provide varying rooms, with high-standard furnishings and fittings in excellent taste. The bar, lounge and breakfast area are in a separate purpose-built structure flanking the large pool. Heating but only fans, no air conditioning. You're paying for the exclusivity – better value out of peak season. Open March–October. 10 rooms.

THE WEST

Akrotiri Beach Hotel €€€ *Paleokastrítsa; tel: 26630 41237/ winter 26610 46500; fax: 26630 41277/winter 26610 20708; <www.akrotiri-beach.com>. A class/4-star.* This modern five-storey resort hotel, renovated in 1997, stands on a headland overlooking the sea and offers high quality air-conditioned rooms, all with verandas looking onto the sea. Facilities include two swimming pools, tennis courts, restaurants, bars and shops. 127 rooms.

Ermones Beach Hotel €€–€€€ (half board) *Érmones; tel: 26610 94241, fax: 26610 94248; <www.sunmarotelermones.gr>. A class/ 4-star.* This bungalow-style hotel enjoys a spectacular setting as it spills down hillside terraces high above Érmones Bay. Its three levels are linked by a funicular-style lift to restaurants and pool above and beach below. A good choice for sporty types, with tennis and water sports available and Corfu's golf course just five minutes away by car. All rooms have excellent views; the hotel is cleverly designed so that other rooms are out of sight, even when you are on your own balcony. 275 rooms.

Fundana Villas €–€€ *Turn at Km 17 of Kérkyra–Paleokastrítsa onto 2-km (1¼mile) side road; tel: 26630 22532; fax: 26630 22453; <www.fundanavillas.com>. A class/4-star.* Another 1980s restoration inn, this time converted from a 17th-century manor, with a commanding ridgetop position in the middle of a gorgeous landscape. Units, from double studios to family apartments, are all different, but most have brick-and-flagstone floors; several apartments were added next to the pool in 2002. Active types can follow part of the recently marked Corfu Trail, which passes right by. Open April–October. 14 units.

Levant Hotel €€–€€€ *Above Pélekas, right beside 'Kaiser's Throne'; tel: 26610 94230; fax: 26610 94115; <www.levant hotel.com>. A class/4-star.* A 1990s-built hotel in mock-traditional style, with superb panoramic views both east and west over the island. Rooms are wood-floored, baths marble-trimmed, ground-floor common areas faux-rustic. There's a small pool, but with some of the island's best beaches a few kilometres (a mile or so) away, you probably won't be using it. Restaurant, bar and lounge with satellite TV. Open April–October. 25 rooms.

Louis Grand Hotel Glyfáda Beach €€€€ *Glyfáda; tel: 26610 94141; fax: 26610 94146; <www.louishotels.com>. A class/4-star.* This outstanding property, right on Glyfáda Beach, is one of the island's best hotels. The furnishings are sumptuous and the décor is a tasteful mix of antique and modern furniture. Facilities include a pool, small lawn and playground, two restaurants, bar, disco and live music. 236 rooms and 15 suites. Open April–October.

Pelecas Country Club €€€€ *Km 8 of Kérkyra–Pélekas road; tel: 26610 52239; fax: 26610 52919; <www.country-club.gr>. A class/4-star.* As the name implies, Corfu's most exclusive rural hotel, occupying an 18th-century mansion and set in over 24 hectares (60 acres) of landscaped grounds. Outbuildings such as the stables, olive press and cellars have been converted into self-catering studios and suites. Stylish breakfasts in the central refectory, pool, tennis courts, helipad for the arrival of the beautiful people. 11 studios and suites. Open April–October.

PAXI

Paxos Club Apartments Hotel €€–€€€€ *Gáïos; tel: 26620 32450; fax: 26620 32097. B class/3-star.* Set in an olive grove 2km (1.2 miles) outside Gáïos Town, this stylish small hotel has been sensitively built around a century-old traditional island house, which is now used as the restaurant (the food is excellent). There's a lovely pool in front, a Jacuzzi, piano bar and children's playground. All rooms are spacious and air-conditioned with a kitchenette and a balcony or patio. 23 apartments. Open May–October.

Recommended Restaurants

Restaurants in resort areas are typically open only during the tourist season (April to October). Those in Kérkyra Town are open all year round, but many of them shut on Sunday.

Unless otherwise indicated, traditional establishments generally open for lunch from noon until around 3.30pm and for dinner from 7pm to around 11.30pm. More tourist-oriented establishments might open early for breakfast or coffee and stay open throughout the day.

Specific times and days of closing below are for summer season, so if you are planning a special journey to dine during low season, it's always advisable to call to confirm. Reservations are necessary only at top restaurants in high season or on Sunday at lunchtime, when Corfiot families eat out en masse. If a telephone number is not provided, it is because reservations are not taken. Staff at a typical taverna will usually bring out more tables and chairs rather than turn you away.

The following prices reflect the average cost of a two-course meal (per person) and a half bottle of wine. The most expensive restaurants add a service charge to your bill (usually around 10 percent), but the vast majority of restaurants do not. However, at all restaurants an automatic tax of 18 percent (VAT) is always included in the prices listed on the menu. It is customary to leave an additional five to 10 percent for the waiter, especially if they're an employee and not the owner.

€€€   over 28 euros
€€   17–28 euros
€   below 17 euros

KERKYRA TOWN

Aegli €€ *Kapodistriou 23; tel: 26610 31949.* Open daily all day. This smart, 1812-established restaurant faces the Listón (with tables also on Kapodistríou Street) and offers a good range of typical Corfiot cooking and international dishes to suit all budgets and tastes.

Start with aubergine (eggplant) croquettes and cheese rolls, then try the rooster stew, fish in red sauce *(bourdétto)* or lamb with vegetables. Quick and efficient service. Major credit cards.

Art Gallery Café € *Gardens off east wing of Palace of St Michael and St George*. No reservations. Open daily 9am–8pm. Tucked away on a quiet terrace by the Municipal Art Gallery, this is the perfect spot to rest while sightseeing or as a prelude to an evening out. Drinks and snacks only. Temporary art exhibitions held upstairs. Cash only.

La Cucina €€ *Gylford 15; tel: 26610 45029*. Open daily 7pm–midnight Feb–Nov. Fight for a table outside at this competent Italian, which does excellent pizzas and handmade pasta dishes – though the interior salon is extremely pleasant in the cooler months. Cash only.

To Dimarchio €€€ *Platía Dimarchíou (Town Hall Square); tel: 26610 39031*. Open daily noon–midnight. The menu balances Greek, Italian and French creations, though the wine list is brief; indoor winter saloon, or umbrella-covered terrace seating on the plaza. Somewhere for a special treat. Credit cards.

La Famiglia €€ *Maniarízi & Arlióti 30, alley between Filellínon and Nikifórou Theotóki; tel: 26610 30270*. Open 8pm–12.30am Mon–Sat. Greek/Italian-run bistro specialising in salads, pasta, lasagne and Italian puddings. Excellent value and efficient service; limited seating, so reservations always essential. Cash only.

Khrysi (O Ninos) € *Sevastianoú 44*. No reservations. Open daily noon–late. The best budget feed in Kérkyra Town: assorted traditional estiatório casserole dishes, plus the best take-away *ghýros* and *souvláki*. Limited sidewalk tables and a stuffy interior make this a better bet for the off-season. Cash only.

Khryssomallis (Babis) € *Nikifórou Theotókou 6; tel: 26610 30342*. Open daily noon–11.30pm. The sign says *zythopsitopolío* ('beer-hall-grill'), but it's also about the last traditional oven-food place in the Old Town: stews, *hórta*, *mousakás*, lamb offal and so forth, all washed down with smooth but potent red wine. From the outside tables on the street you can just see the Listón. The Durrells ate here during their 1930s stay; the restaurant has been around a lot longer. Cash only.

Mouragia €–€€ *Arseníou 15, north quay; tel: 26610 33815*. Open noon–12.30am. A good mix of seafood (with fresh and frozen items clearly indicated) and Corfiot *mayireftá* such as *sofríto* and *pastitsáda*. Inexpensive for any island, let alone Corfu, and great sea views into the bargain.

Paradosiakor € *Solomoú 20, Spiliá*. Open daily noon–11pm. The lower end of Solomoú Street is a good place to come for authentic Greek cooking on a budget. Make your choice from a variety of daily specials, all simmering under the glass counter. Cash only.

Pende Aderfes € *Xenofóndos Stratigoú 151, Mandoúki; tel: 26610 38263*. Open from lunch until 1.30am. This basic little grill with seating out on a flagstoned patio is the most established of several hereabouts. Menu strictly of salads, chops, sausage and *kondosoúvli*, washed down by beer and bulk wine. Some of the 'five sisters' of the name wait on you; Spyridoula in particular is a character, with a voice that can probably be heard in Albania.

Il Pollo € *Mitropoliton Athanasiou 71, Garitsa Bay; tel: 26610 26210*. Open daily 6.30pm–late and Sunday lunch Apr–June. Set back from the seafront, behind a green parallel to the coast road, this lively Greek taverna is popular with the locals for its charcoal grills and traditional dishes.

Rex €€–€€€ *Kapodistríou 66; tel: 26610 39649*. Open all day daily. Established in 1932, the Rex is something of a Kérkyra Town institution. It serves a wide range of Corfiot, Greek and northern European cuisine. Major credit cards.

Tenedos €€ *Solomoú 5, Spiliá district; tel: 26610 36277*. Open Mon–Sat, noon until late. Charming little restaurant on the steps leading to the New Fort, this informal alfresco spot is right by the bright-pink Panagía Tenédou. The owners are French and Greek;

perhaps not surprisingly, the food is a mix of international and local dishes. Leave room for a delicious homemade fruit pie. Live music nightly; half-price meals for children. Major credit cards.

Theotoki Brothers (Kerkyraïki Paradosiaki Taverna) € *Alkiviádi Dári 69, Garítsa Bay.* Open daily noon–4.30pm and 7–11.30pm. By far the best of the half-dozen tavernas with tables out in the eucalyptus park here. A full range of *mayirevtá* dishes and grills, plus some seafood, issue from an incredibly narrow kitchen, at very reasonable prices. Service can be leisurely, even by Corfu standards.

Venetian Well €€€ *Platía Kremastí, northeast of Orthodox Cathedral, Campiello district; tel: 26610 44761.* Open lunch and 7–11pm Mon–Sat Mar–Oct. Tucked away through an arch, with tables set around the eponymous well, is some of the town's most innovative and expensive cuisine – generic Aegean with interesting twists. Recipes change seasonally, depending on the proprietor's winter travels and inspiration: past dishes have included duck in plum sauce or *dolmádes* with wild rice. Excellent (and pricy) wine list. Credit cards.

THE SOUTH

Alonaki Bay € *Paralía Alonáki, near Korissíon Lagoon and Gardíki Castle; tel: 26610 75872.* Open lunch and dinner. Good country recipes, strong on vegetables and seafood – beans, greens, scorpion-fish soup – at shady tables on a terrace overlooking the sea. Locals usually outnumber tourists here – one of the best endorsements. Cash only.

Boúkari Beach €–€€ *Boúkari, 4km (2½ miles) beyond Mesongí; tel: 26620 51791.* The best of the seafood tavernas along this seashore hamlet, in an idyllic setting, with patently fresh fare at some of the most attractive prices on the island. Cash only.

Trypas €€€ *Kinopiástes, en route to Achilleion, 7km (4½ miles) southwest of Kérkyra; tel: 26610 56333.* Open daily supper only; closed mid-Nov–mid-Dec. Classic if rather touristy taverna in an old farmhouse that has been patronised by many notables. The set-price menu of Corfiot dishes should offer something for everyone's taste. Greek folk dancing most summer evenings. Credit cards.

NORTH OF KERKYRA TOWN

Etrusco €€€ *Káto Korakiána village, on the road down to Dassiá;* tel: 26610 93342. Open Apr–Oct, supper only. Top-calibre nouvelle Italian cooking by father, son and spouses, served in a carefully restored country manor. Specialities including *timpano parpadellas* (pasta with duck and truffles) and a 200-label wine list don't come cheap, but this has been ranked as one of the best five Greek tavernas outside of Athens. Reserve at least two weeks in advance. Credit cards.

Limeri €€ *Káto Korakiána village, at Y-junction just above the Kastello;* tel: 26610 93736. This taverna is best for its *mezédes* plates like asparagus *demáti* (in cream sauce) and fried oyster mushrooms; also there's the usual range of oven dishes and grills. Good bulk wine and desserts, friendly service. Credit cards.

THE NORTHEAST

Agni €€ *Agní cove;* tel: 26630 91142. Open for lunch and dinner Apr–Oct. The romance of the proprietors – she's Greek, he's English – has been the basis of British newspaper features and a BBC documentary, but beyond the media hype the food is very good, and reflects the meeting of cultures: stuffed sardines, garlic prawns, mussels in wine and herbs. The pebble-cove setting is idyllic, but parking is limited (you can come by excursion boat). Credit cards.

Cavo Barbaro (Fotis) €€ *Avláki beach, east of Kassiópi;* tel: 26630 81905. Open daily all day May–Oct. An unusually good beach taverna, with welcoming service. A few *magirevtá* dishes at lunch, like risotto and *soudzoukákia*; more grills after dark, plus homemade *glyká koutalioú* (candied fruit). There's seating on the lawn and plenty of parking. The only thing 'barbarous' here can be the wind, as there's no shelter; check direction and strength before heading downhill. Cash only.

Kouloúra €€ *Kouloúra cove; tel: 26630 91253.* Open daily all day Apr–Oct. Fairly priced seafood or fish, large selection of *mezédes* and salads, plus unusually elaborate pies at this impeccably set taverna overlooking one of the most photogenic anchorages on Corfu. Credit cards; reservations needed in peak season.

Little Italy €€ *Kassiopí, opposite Grivas supermarket; tel: 26630 81749.* Open daily 6pm–late. Jolly *trattoria* in an old stone house run by Italian brothers. The fare includes salmon in pastry parcels, pizza, pastas smothered in freshly made sauces. Cash only.

Mitsos €€ *Nisáki, on the Mitsos rock outcrop; tel: 26630 91240.* Open all day Apr–Oct. This ordinary-looking beachside taverna stands out for the cheerful service from the two partners, plus rapid turnover and thus freshness of the fare, which includes fried local fish and well-executed *sofríto*. Cash only.

Toula €€ *Agní cove; tel: 26630 91350.* Open for lunch and supper Apr–Oct, also winter weekends. Worth a special mention for its professional demeanour, nice line in hot *mezédes* and the house special *garídes Toula* – grilled prawns with spicy mixed-rice pilaff. Any of the seafood main dishes, washed down by excellent bulk white wine, is a likely winner here. Credit cards.

THE NORTH AND NORTHWEST

Akroghiali €€€ *Far south end of the bay, Ágios Geórgios north; tel: 697 7334278.* Open daily Jun–Oct. A bumpy, wash-out-prone track leads 1,500m (1,640yds) south from the beach to this little eyrie (marked by a windmill) run by a local lad and his Dutch partner. The fish is excellent, as are the *mezédes*, but as ever confirm on-scale weight before proceeding. Cash only.

Foros € *Paleá Períthia; tel: 26630 98373.* Open daily May–Oct. One of the first tavernas in this once-deserted Venetian village, operating out of a restored house. Fare is basic – grills, salads, local cheese, *píttes* (turnovers), a dish of the day – but so are the prices. Cash only.

Ftelia (Elm Tree) € *Strinýlas village plaza; tel: 26630 71454.* Open lunch and dinner May–Oct, random days in winter. An almost mandatory stop on the way to or from the summit of Mt Pandokrátor, this taverna specialises in game (venison, wild boar), unusual starters such as snails or artichoke pie, apple pie and proper Dutch coffee. Cash only.

Invisible Kitchen €€ *Acharávi; tel: 26630 98051, 697 6652933; <www.theinvisiblekitchen.co.uk>.* Open late Apr–mid-Oct. Not a restaurant as such, but a catering service – young British chefs Ben and Claudia will deliver ready meals for your villa party, from light bites to elaborate feasts. Nouvelle Italian, French, Thai, Indian, Chinese or Greek menus (from €22.50 each, minimum four diners) – and the food is to die for.

7th Heaven Bar/Panorama Restaurant € *Longás Beach, Peroulátes; tel: 26630 95035.* Open all day May–Oct. This is one of the best places from which to watch Corfu's majestic sunset; by half an hour before the event, it's standing-room only for a mixed crowd, who are treated to a good range of ambient music by staff. If you linger after dark, the Panorama serves up good, standard Greek fare. Cash only.

PAXI

La Rosa di Paxos €€–€€€ *Lákka port quay; tel: 26620 31471.* Open for lunch and supper, May–Oct. The Greco-Italian management is reflected in the blend of flavours in the seafood, pasta and other generic Mediterranean dishes. The place for a last-night treat. Credit cards.

Vassilis (Kostakis) €€ *Longós quay; tel: 26620 31587.* Open for lunch and supper, May–Oct. Now often known by its alias – Kostakis – after the son who's taken it over, this has grown from a grilled-fish specialist to an all-round taverna with imaginative recipes like stuffed mushrooms and peppers, baked-meat dishes and various oven pies. Occasionally hosts live music at Sunday lunch. Credit cards.

INDEX